ALEKSANDR GRIN: THE FORGOTTEN VISIONARY

Aleksandr Grin in 1908. (A gift from a private collection.)

Russian Biography Series, No. 7

Nicholas J.L. Luker

ALEKSANDR GRIN:
THE FORGOTTEN VISIONARY

Oriental Research Partners
Newtonville, Mass.
1980

ISBN 0-89250-137-5 (cloth)

For a detailed brochure on
the Russian Biography
Series, of which this volume
is number 7 of
twenty-five so far
scheduled, please write to
Dr. P. Clendenning, Editor,
ORP, Box 158, Newtonville,
Mass. 02160.

To my son,
Nathaniel Max,
bringer of joy out of sorrow

CONTENTS

ILLUSTRATIONS

PREFACE

This book is based on parts of a doctoral thesis on Aleksandr Grin accepted by the University of Nottingham, England, in 1971. Drawing on archive and memoir material, it aims to examine Grin's life in detail and to correct popular misconceptions about him—notably that he was a seafaring desperado who skilfully plagiarised the work of Western adventure writers. At the same time it touches on his posthumous literary fate and seeks briefly to define his significance for Russian letters.

There is no complete edition of Grin's works. The most comprehensive collection currently available is the six-volume *Sobranie sochinenii* published in Moscow in 1965 by "Pravda" (Biblioteka "Ogonëk"), and reference is made to this edition wherever possible. All translations from the Russian, whether from published or unpublished sources, are my own.

I must acknowledge a profound debt of gratitude to several friends in the Soviet Union whose assistance in the preparation of this work has been invaluable. Not only did they generously allow me access to privately-held material, the original manuscripts of which the State archives declined to release, but also gave me immense help and unremitting hospitality. Sadly, of course, they must remain nameless.

In addition, I wish to express my thanks to Dorothy Honniball of Nottingham University Library, who typed my manuscript with her usual efficiency and care; to Garth Terry, Slavonic Librarian at the University of Nottingham, for his assistance in obtaining research material and his advice on bibliographical matters; to Professor Marcus Wheeler of the Queen's University of Belfast for his helpful suggestions about aspects of Grin's work; and to Dr. Philip Clendenning, Editor of this biography, who has advised me throughout the writing of it.

I would also like to record my deep gratitude to the late Max Hayward, Fellow of St. Antony's College, Oxford, for his abiding interest in my work on Grin and for his unstinting encouragement ever since I embarked on it—at his suggestion—as a post-graduate. His enthusiastic support and expert guidance have meant more to me than I can possibly say.

Lastly, I wish to thank my wife, Patricia, and my son, Nathaniel, for the tolerance that they show towards a husband and father who is all too often closeted in his study. Without their patience and kindness this biography would never have been.

NICHOLAS LUKER

Grassington,
North Yorkshire,
England

   1979

CHAPTER I

THE EARLY YEARS
1880-1910
VAGRANT AND AGITATOR

> "Few know how I spent my youth;
> all the same, it was not easy!"
>   A. S. Grin[1]

Such sources of information about Aleksandr Grin's biography as exist are few and seldom objective. Several short, unpublished manuscripts of reminiscences about Grin by friends and acquaintances survive, in either archives or private hands in the Soviet Union, but these are of little value in creating a complete picture of his life. Though neither deals with the whole of Grin's life, the longer memoirs by Vera Pavlovna Kalitskaia and Nina Nikolaevna Grin—the author's first and second wives respectively—are far more valuable, but it was not until late 1972 that parts of these manuscripts were published for the first time.[2] Information about Grin's childhood and youth is very scanty, and for this one must rely almost entirely on his own record, the *Autobiographical Tale (Avtobiograficheskaia povest')*, the bulk of which was first published in the Moscow journal *Zvezda* ("The Star") in 1931, only a year before his death.[3] But even this, written hurriedly and purely for financial reasons, was never intended by its author to be a strictly factual, documentary account of his life. It is full of subjective observations and digressions, and contains several inaccuracies of both chronology and event. Since the *Tale* breaks off in October 1905, the events of Grin's life after that become still more difficult to trace. The eight years between his separation from his first wife in 1913 and his second marriage in 1921 are especially vague. As Nina Grin recalls in her memoirs, Grin was always loath to speak of himself and his past, even to those close to him, and had a profound aversion for direct disclosure of biographical details in his work, though these are often to be found in an indirect form. To editors asking for biographical information, he would reply simply: "My biography is in my books . . . one only has to know how to read them."[4]

Aleksandr Stepanovich Grinevskii was born on 23 August 1880 (N.S.) in the district town of Slobodskoi, about thirty kilometres east of Viatka, now Kirov. His father, Stefan Evzebievich (in popular speech Stepan Evseevich) Grinevskii was of Polish birth and in 1862, at the age of nineteen, had been arrested for alleged seditious activities.[5] Grin always liked to think that his father had taken part in the Polish rebellion of 1863, but this was not the case. While a pupil in the top class at the *gimnaziia* in Vitebsk, he became a member of a rebellious group consisting, it seems, largely of schoolboys. After a trial he was exiled on 4 September 1864, to the north of Tomsk Province and deprived of personal rights. After spending three years in the remote Siberian town of Kolyvan' (near the modern Novosibirsk), in 1867 as exile No. 1578 he was transferred to Viatka Province.[6] On 15 September 1872, Grinevskii married Anna Stepanovna Liapkova, a native of Viatka descended from a Russified Swede, Lepke, who had been a prisoner-of-war under Peter the Great. Konstantin Paustovskii has given a brief picture of Stefan Grinevskii: " . . . in exile he quickly became Russified, married, reared a large family, began to drink, and led the life of a hopeless failure. The youth full of noble impulses was rapidly transformed into a petty official in the administration of Viatka's benevolent institutions."[7] Grin's sisters, Ekaterina Stepanovna Malovechkina and Angelina Stepanovna Podvysotskaia, have, however, denied the widely-held belief that their father was a drunkard who died in poverty: "Our father . . . was a man who had suffered for the idea of freedom . . . a man of great intelligence and extreme fairness, sympathy and goodness."[8]

In Slobodskoi Stefan Grinevskii worked in the office of a brewery, but later in Viatka became first a clerk and then a self-taught accountant in the *zemstvo* hospital, a position he held until his death in 1913. Before Aleksandr was born, the couple adopted an orphan girl, Natalia. The boy was two when his parents moved from Slobodskoi to Viatka, and he said later that this winter journey by sledge under a brilliant, starry sky—his first childhood recollection—awoke in him his lifelong pensiveness and love of the beautiful.

The young Grinevskii did not attend primary school, as he was taught to read, write and count at home. The first book he read was Swift's *Gulliver's Travels*, at the age of five, and it was in these earliest years that the inventive dreamer was born. His reading was haphazard, an escape and an adventure in itself. He was a curiously adult, contemplative child, who concocted chemical mixtures and dreamed of discovering the Philosopher's Stone. Perhaps his intelligence and imagination had already made him old before his time. "I well remember," he writes, "that books written specially for children did not satisfy me."[9] Mayne Reid and Gustave Aimard were his constant companions, and his passion for reading to the exclusion of everything else was to affect his studies as he moved through school.

At the age of eight the boy read for the first time the fairy-story *Mila and Nolli (Mila i Nolli)* by N. P. Wagner, who wrote under the pseudonym of "Kot-Murlyka." As he said to Nina Grin many years later, the tale made a profound impression on him and affected not only the subsequent choice of heroines in his works but also his relationships with women throughout his life. The story of Mila's boundless love for Nolli, first her childhood friend and then her beloved, determined Grin's whole conception of happiness. From the age of eight the boy began to yearn for such a love and continued to do so for most of his adult years: "I did not realise what had happened to me when I read this tale. I did not understand at the time the word 'love' nor all that went with it, but my child's soul began to pine. . . . I said to myself, as it were: 'I want a love like that for myself!' This was the first knock at the door of my feelings as a man. Later I learnt about Kot-Murlyka. . . . who had so opportunely spoken to me a true, poetic word when I was a child. It was to me like the words of Egl' were to the little Assol'.[10] I grew up, and life pounded, frayed and tormented me, but the image of Mila did not die. Instead, it kept on growing in my soul and in my notion of happiness."[11]

In 1889, at the age of nine, the boy was put into the preparatory class of the Viatka district grammar school, the *Aleksandrovskoe zemskoe real'noe uchilishche*. Whilst his fine memory and vivid imagination enabled him to shine in history, geography and religious knowledge, his frequently rather unsystematic thinking meant that he fared badly in mathematics, French and German. His behaviour left much to be desired. "Grinevskii is a capable boy and has an excellent memory," his teachers said of him, "but he is . . . a mischievous child, a madcap, an imp."[12] In the journal of the school inspector for the years 1890-93 the boy's name appears rather often. For example: "19 March 1890: clapped his hands when the master on duty failed to read the prayer correctly, and in the same way annoyed the scripture teacher; 7 May 1890: behaved improperly during religious knowledge lessons and was sent out of the class."[13] A report given to the boy by the pedagogical council, as well as class journals preserved in the Viatka archives, show that most subjects did not prove beyond him at all, despite what he himself may say about school in his *Autobiographical Tale*. But he was a wilful child who exasperated his teachers. He was often punished and his conduct mark never rose above a modest "three."

The solitariness which became so much a part of the Grin legend later in his life seems to have been the product both of an introverted temperament and of an innate ability to find entertainment and satisfaction within himself. As later in adult life, so now in childhood he had few friends—"I preferred to play alone. . . ."[14] So vivid was his imagination, so impassioned his dreamings, that they filled much of his childhood, as in a more sophisticated way they were to dominate his adult years. The bedrock of his invented, sub-tropical *Grinlandia*[15] was laid down here in the kitchen garden of the child's home in Viatka. As Grin recalled later: "Perpetually I could see in my imagination the forests of America, the jungles of Africa and the taiga of Siberia. The words Orinoco, Mississippi and Sumatra rang like music in my ears."[16] The experiences of adulthood were to help him realise in his writing the aspirations so keenly felt in these earliest years: "What I read in books, even if it were the cheapest fiction, was for me always an agonisingly longed-for reality."[17]

His constant thirst for novelty explains the lack of system and the hurried carelessness which, as he confesses, characterised his childhood pursuits. It was as if his imagination and invention went leaping off ahead of his hands. " . . . interested in many things, snatching at everything yet completing nothing, and being impatient, impassioned and careless, I achieved perfection in nothing, always compensating for my insufficiencies with dreams."[18]

1891 brought suspension from school for poor conduct, followed by expulsion twelve months later. In the lower classes the boy had gained a reputation as a composer of satirical verses, and now his satires and caricatures proved too much for the school authorities. The inspector's journal for the school year 1892-93 contains the entry: "14 October: during the German lesson wrote improper verses about the inspector, his assistants and the teachers. Drew caricatures during the arithmetic lesson."[19] The "improper verses" were written in imitation of Pushkin's poem *A Collection of Insects (Sobranie nasekomykh)* (1829), and pilloried each of the staff in turn. Though the pedagogical council was inclined to look indulgently upon the affair, the school inspector remained adamant, and in October 1892, the boy was duly expelled. Since the Viatka *gimnaziia* refused to take him, he was forced to enter the municipal school, the *gorodskoe uchilishche*, instead. This was the first setback in a life that was to be all too full of them.

In 1893, when Aleksandr was twelve, his mother died of tuberculosis at the age of thirty-seven. Life had been neither particularly happy nor easy for the family while she was alive: the father's salary had remained the same, while new children were born (there were two younger daughters, Ekaterina and Angelina, as well as the older adopted one, Natalia, and an infant son, Boris); the mother was ill, the father drank, and the debts grew. "Taking everything into account, it was a hard, drab life," Grin wrote later. "While mother was alive I grew up amidst wretched surroundings, without any proper guidance whatsoever; but when she died things became far worse. . . ."[20] His father soon took a second wife— the widow of a psalm-reader, L. A. Boretskaia, who brought her nine year-old son, Pavel, to join the family. There seems to have been no love lost between Aleksandr and his stepmother, and he always remembered her as malicious and cold.

In his early teens the boy developed a passion for hunting. Armed with an old ram-rod rifle given him by his father, he roamed the forests around Viatka, revelling in his freedom and solitude. In his *Tale* Grin examines in retrospect the reasons why he so enjoyed hunting: "I . . . liked the element of hazard, of chance; for that reason I made no attempt to acquire a dog."[21] More than all the varied beauty and scents of the forest, he liked the excitement of unexpected discovery—"I loved to seek and suddenly find."[22] It was the atmosphere and associations of hunting that he enjoyed, rather than the development and exercise of acquired skills. Yet his characteristic carelessness was apparent here too, he recalls, for he loaded his rifle hurriedly and aimed indiscriminately at any bird.

Occasionally during these years he would write poetry and send it to the weekly journals *Niva* ("The Corn-field") and *Rodina* ("The Motherland"), but never received any reply. His juvenilia were evidently inspired by current literary fashion and mood, for he recalls: "My poems were about shattered dreams and hopelessness, loneliness and gloom—exactly the kind of verses which filled the weeklies at the time. Anyone would have thought they were the work of a forty year-old Chekhovian hero, not of a boy aged between eleven and fifteen."[23] With surprise Grin also recalls an article he wrote while in the fifth class of his second school, entitled "The Harmfulness of Mayne Reid and Gustave Aimard" *("Vred Main-Rida i Gustava Emara")*. So obvious to him is its thesis now that he fails to understand why he ever wrote it: "I developed an idea about the destructive effect those writers have upon the young. My conclusion was this: having read their fill of picturesque pages about mysterious, distant continents, children despise their ordinary surroundings, pine and long to run away to America. As a parallel I suggested a theatre performance, after which the dwelling and lot of the poor man seem more unenviable and gloomy still."[24] Fortunately, the boy's years at his second school passed without major incident, and when he left, he was awarded a final conduct mark of "five"–"so as not to mar my life."[25]

Inspired by the example of a young relative on his mother's side who had become a sailor, Aleksandr now resolved to go to sea. But when he met the man in question, he was astonished at the discrepancy between this real sailor and his ideal of the seafarer, a romantic image drawn from authors such as Captain Marryat, Mayne Reid and Fenimore Cooper. The mariner did not even *look* right for the part, he recalls, for he was "clumsy, unpleasantly broad-shouldered, swarthy, handsome in a sickly way, and obtuse; and to crown it all, he had become a customs officer."[26] Grin adds that the man was not a real sailor in his eyes, because he sailed only "on a closed sea" (*"v zakrytom more"*)[27] [i.e., on the Black Sea], a remark strongly reminiscent of the heated debates between lake and ocean sailor in Fenimore Cooper's *The Pathfinder*, a novel with which the young Grinevskii was almost certainly familiar in translation. Disillusionment was the result of a meeting with another sailor too, for the latter's preoccupation with practical matters hobbled the boy's galloping romantic dreams. "I was interested in impressions of distant lands, storms and battles with pirates," he writes, "but he talked about rations, pay and the cheapness of water-melons."[28] However, the spring of 1895 brought fresh vigour to his romantic notions, when on the river landing-stage of Viatka he beheld two naval cadets from the Black Sea Fleet cruisers *Ochakov* and *Sevastopol'*. "I gazed like one bewitched," he remembers, "at these visitors from a beautiful world that to me was full of mystery. I was not envious of them. Instead, I felt rapture and yearning."[29]

Later Grin admitted that the drab environment of Viatka served to heighten the fancied exoticism of a life at sea. Feeling so much a part of that environment, he seemed insignificant before denizens of the desired, other world. As he explains in his *Tale*: "To understand this, one must be familiar with the provincial way of life [*byt*] of that time, the life of a God-forsaken town. This atmosphere of strained mistrustfulness, false pride and shame is best conveyed by Chekhov's story *My Life* [*Moia zhizn'*]. When I read this tale it was just as if I were reading about Viatka."[30]

In the summer of 1896, when he was fifteen, Aleksandr decided to set off for Odessa to become a sailor. A steamer was due to leave Viatka for Kazan' on 23 June and the boy's father gave him twenty-five roubles for the journey. As he had never left Viatka before, it is not surprising that the prospect of travelling 2,000 versts made him apprehensive. During his last days at home, he remembers, his stepmother was more friendly towards him, almost as if she welcomed his departure. When his father saw him off from the landing-stage, the boy felt that his first real adventure had begun: "I was both jubilant and sad. I was dreaming of the sea, covered with sails. . . ."[31]

The first three days of his journey, to Kazan', were a kaleidoscope of impressions and sensations. Via Nizhnii Novgorod he reached Moscow, where he was to catch the train for Odessa. Having only ever read of locomotives in books, he was astonished at their smallness, since he had always imagined them as high as bell-towers. His confidence was shaken by the contrast between Viatka and Moscow, and he became very suspicious and shy. "In comparison with quiet, little Viatka," he recalls, "the world of energetic, noisy, . . . bustling people made me feel timid; in almost everyone I met I imagined a rogue."[32] Believing he would be taken on immediately as a sailor in Odessa, he freely spent what little money he had, telling everybody he was going to sea. Though longing to be independent and already considering himself grown up, he was later to be very glad of a letter of introduction from a fellow-passenger to Nikolai Khokhlov, a book-keeper with the Russian Steam-Navigation and Trade Company *(Russkoe Obshchestvo Parokhodstva i Torgovli)* (ROPT) in Odessa.

Reaching Odessa two days later, he ran to catch his first glimpse of the sea. In his *Tale* thirty-five years afterwards, Grin described his impressions thus: ". . . astounded, I stopped: below me, to left and right, thundered the harbour at midday. Smoke, sails, ships, trains, steamers, masts, the dark blue roadstead,—everything was there and it was impossible to take it all in at once. . . . the faintly misty expanse of ocean stood vertical, like a wall, and over the top of this wall crawled the long smoke-trail of a vessel hidden by the distance. Not for several minutes did my eyes become accustomed to the spectacle. The only thing that bewildered me was to see the horizon much nearer than I had expected; I had always thought that the ocean's distance stretched a great deal further."[33] But after dreaming for so long of the sea as the well-spring of exoticism and excitement, he felt instant disenchantment: "this new world evidently had no need of me at that moment. . . ."[34] The final communion was still to come, though, for he was as yet only looking at the sea from a distance. In the dusk, agitated and trembling, "as if going to make a declaration of love,"[35] he made his way down to the port itself. Once more, however, he was filled with the feeling that he was superfluous and out of place. "I breathed in the fascination of the sea, full of wonders at every step, but everything around me overwhelmed me with the force of its grandiose, picturesque completeness; amidst all this I felt unnecessary and alien."[36]

Possessing no sailing experience whatsoever, he found it impossible to secure work on a ship, and was soon destitute and starving. Only whei things had come to this pass did he decide to make use of the hitherto despised letter of introduction to Khokhlov. His appearance at the ROPT office created a sensation. He was put into a sailors' boarding-house while Khokhlov and his friends tried to find him work among captains of their acquaintance. Meanwhile he continued to roam the port in search of a job. He was promised work on a tanker but arrived late to find that his place had been taken by someone else. As things turned out, his delay probably saved his life, since the vessel sank in the English Channel *en route* to Petersburg.

At the end of August 1896, his luck turned and he was taken on as an apprentice by the *Plato*, a coaster owned by the Russian Transport Company *(Rossiiskoe Obshchestvo Transporta)*. Perhaps more than the average novice, he was the butt of everyone's tricks and practical jokes. His acute sensitivity and vivid imagination, as well as the clear notion of what he was privately searching for, made it difficult for him to come to terms with many aspects of sea life that proved contrary to his expectations: " . . . my inner difference from the other sailors made itself apparent. I was everlastingly absorbed in my own notion of sea life—the same life that I was now actually experiencing. I was naive, knew little about people and did not know how to live in the way that those around me lived. I . . . was not strong, not quick-witted."[37] His childhood predilection for outward impressions rather than for a deeper understanding of things was still characteristic of him now. Nevertheless, his first sight of the open sea as they sailed to Sevastopol' brought him immense enjoyment. The *Plato* called at all Crimean ports to load and unload cargo, but Grinevskii could not help with the work for he was not strong enough. This first voyage made an indelible impression on him, and features of the Crimean coast seen during the course of it were to emerge years later in his *Grinlandia*. A striking example was the spectacle of Yalta at night amid the sounds of orchestral music and the scent of flowers, a scene that provides the backdrop for the carnival in the novel *She Who Runs on the Waves (Begushchaia po volnam)* (1928).[38]

Though under threat of being put ashore because he was unable to pay for his keep, the youth managed to make another round trip on the *Plato*, through Sevastopol', Kerch, Batumi and Feodosia, before returning to Odessa. There he was finally dismissed and was again obliged to turn for help to Khokhlov, who installed him in the boarding-house once more. But after only a month, a disagreement with his benefactor forced him to leave this comfortable refuge, whereupon the condition of sores on his legs brought a fortnight's stay in the local hospital. His description of this unhygienic institution and the practical jokes of its more robust inmates is both horrifying and hilarious.[39] When his legs improved, he left the loathsome place with great relief.

But his ill-fed, jobless existence went on as before—"I starved systematically,"[40] he writes—and for two weeks he wandered round Odessa, begging for food and collecting scrap iron. Then he was offered a job on the *Saint Nicholas*, a coaster carrying tiles to Kherson. He helped with the loading of cargo and acted as ship's cook, while the vessel's owner cursed him for his lack of skill. Arriving in Kherson, he decided he would not work his return passage under such bad conditions, and left the ship. Returning to Odessa, he went again to Khokhlov for help, and though the latter now washed his hands of him, his colleague, Silant'ev, was most generous, giving the youth clothes, food and money, and finding him work as a *markirovshchik* in a warehouse—a job that involved directing the placing of loads brought in by stevedores. Silant'ev's generosity was to be poeticised later in Grin's last completed novel, *The Road to Nowhere (Doroga nikuda)* (1930), where the young hero, Davenant, is fed, clothed and helped by his benefactor, Futroz.[41]

The early spring of 1897 saw the only voyage abroad of Grin's life, when he sailed from Odessa to Alexandria on the *Tsarevich*, a cargo vessel owned by the ROPT. During the return journey he was relieved of his duties at Smyrna (Izmir) for refusing to participate in rowing lessons prescribed by the captain, and completed the voyage as a passenger. Once back in Odessa, he lived for a while by selling some of his clothes, then worked as a coal-loader, often spending the night in the port without shelter.

At the beginning of July 1897, he felt the call of home. After working his passage via Rostov to Kalach-on-Don, he reached Tsaritsyn by rail and then sailed as far as Kazan'. The steamer from Kazan' to Viatka ran aground and he had to cover the remaining two hundred versts on foot, in high winds and heavy rain. Arriving home eight days later, he was too proud to tell his father the truth, saying he had travelled the last part of his journey with post-horses. Though he did not realise it, his sailing days were already over.

Till July 1898, he lived at home, taking a variety of jobs which included working as a clerk in a local office and copying out theatre parts. But none satisfied him and he became depressed, feeling that he had "neither place nor occupation in life."[42] The ingrained prejudices, grey atmosphere and desperately unstimulating society of his native town did little to help. Towards the end of July 1898, he set off again, to escape from "dismal, prim Viatka with its doctrine: be like everyone else."[43]

This time he went to Baku, where he spent a wretched year among hobos, thieves and drunks, taking casual jobs in the port whenever he could. At first he had a bed in a room to let, but then was forced to sleep outside, in empty boilers and beneath upturned boats. When the cold weather came, he found a place in a charitable institution where lice and human filth were rife. He engaged in every conceivable device to earn money, gambling with coppers, buying old clothes and trying to sell them at a profit, and writing "begging" letters to compassionate people of the town. Drunkenness, theft and violence constituted his dominant impressions of Baku. The city's dregs peopled the district known as "Forty Taverns" ("Sorok dukhanov") and Grin came to know them intimately, familiar as he was with the cheapest inns and lodging-houses. Objectively and without emotion he describes in his Tale a typical brawl in one of the dukhans: "There began the uproar of a fight which could lead to murder. They struck the man with bottles, with their feet and with a stool; they stabbed him with a fork, gnawed at his ear, tore out his hair and jumped on him. He did not shout but just muttered drunken curses. Finally, one tramp thrust his hand into the man's mouth and ripped it away to the ear which was already barely dangling on a strip of red flesh. Then the police arrived and the victim was taken away by cab."[44]

Because of his poor physical condition and dishevelled appearance, Grinevskii again failed to find work as a sailor. He often resorted to begging, though largely without success, for his shame prevented him from lending conviction to his words. In all, these months were probably the most miserable of his whole life. As he wrote later, this winter in Baku "lasted an endless time . . . the gloom and horror of it often drove me to tears."[45]

In the spring of 1899 he found work for a while as a bellows-operator in a forge. After that, job followed job as before. His visit to the oil-producing town of Balakhany produced so unpleasant an impression on him that, despite the high pay there, he did not seek work, but returned to Baku the following day instead. The sight of the oil-fields, with their ugly derricks and pipelines, as well as the all-pervasive odour of crude oil, strengthened his antipathy for the soullessness of an increasingly industrialised world. In May 1899, he was given a job by fishermen near Baku, where he helped to mend nets and fish for white sturgeon. But an attack of malaria forced him to return to the city, where he spent five days in hospital. Then, together with a fellow-hobo, he set off to tramp the Northern Caucasus, but rapidly grew tired of his companion who was an inveterate beggar and idler. Next he took a job in a bakehouse which involved taking provisions to men building the Baku-Petrovsk railway. He enjoyed the work because he was his own master, but the bakery soon closed down and he was forced to move on. Hearing there were fisheries forty versts away, he set off to walk there along the coast. After a few hours, the intense heat and the agony of thirst caused him to run crying out for help along the shore, and he was lucky to survive. His next job was on a coastal steamer, the *Atrek*, but constant fever soon forced him to give it up.

Now, for the second time, he headed for home. *En route* to Kazan' he was twice put ashore for travelling without a ticket, an experience reflected in his story *Passenger Pyzhikov (Passazhir Pyzhikov)*, first published as *The Stowaway (Zaiats)* (1912).[46] Three days' sailing from Kazan' brought him within sight of Viatka, that "quiet town of my birth, where nothing awaited me but the reproaches and sorrow of my father at my everlasting fecklessness."[47] His second homecoming was a repetition of the first, and again he lied in an attempt to conceal the fact that he was penniless. For the next few months he worked as an attorney's clerk.

In February 1900, he decided to leave for the Urals goldfields. Like his journeys to the south and its sea, this new venture eastwards was inspired by the romantic notions that were his very life-blood: "I dreamed of hunting for treasure, of finding a nugget weighing one and a half poods—in a word, I was still under the influence of Rider Haggard and Gustave Aimard."[48]

He left Viatka on 23 February, and made for the district town of Slobodskoi where he was born. On the way he took shelter for the night in the house of a generous deacon who, as it turned out, shared his guest's

admiration for Aimard. Grin's attempts in Slobodskoi to find his godfather, Tetskii, an exiled Pole like his father, proved fruitless. In Glazov,
190 versts further east, he looked up the inspector of the *gorodskoe
uchilishche*, a certain Petrov, who had taught him in his second school
in Viatka. Here he was well-treated, fed and given a bath. Grin recalls
that when asked by Petrov whether he liked Maxim Gorky's tales, he
defended the writer enthusiastically: "'You mean, you approve?' Petrov asked. As I understood it, this gloomy remark referred not only to
the literary aspects of Gorky's works, but also to the way of life of his
heroes. I answered in the affirmative."[49] The following morning Grinevskii persuaded a railway guard to allow him to travel in an empty goods
truck to Perm', and in the frost of -20°C that night almost froze to death.
In Perm' he visited Rzhevskii, another exiled Pole, to whom his father
had written asking for help in finding his son work. Despite the fact that
his father's ties with other exiles had long been broken, the youth was
fed, given money and found work in the Perm' railway workshops. But
after only two weeks here, Grinevskii decided to leave, for spring was
beginning and he had heard that good money was to be had on the nearest goldfields, those of Count Shuvalov: "I dreamed of camp-fires in the
forest, carbines, the secret dens of hoarders, feasts and gold, bears and
Indians. . . ."[50]

When his naive hopes of instant wealth were not fulfilled, however,
his enthusiasm rapidly waned, and he left the goldfields to work in an
iron foundry. Then in April 1900, he became a lumberjack. It was now
that he met the genial forest giant, his fellow-lumberjack Il'ia, whom he
describes affectionately in his *Tale* and with whom he shared a cabin in
the forest. Though the work of felling was often beyond the youth's
strength, he enjoyed Il'ia's company and in the evenings he would tell
him stories and fairy-tales. Given such an appreciative listener, Grinevskii's fantasy took wing as never before: ". . . as I told my stories, I became carried away with delight. After two weeks I had given him all my
rich store of Perrault, the Brothers Grimm, Afanas'ev and Andersen;
and when the store was exhausted, I began to modify my tales and im-
provise after the manner of Scheherazade."[51] As for life in the forest,
however, he soon became disenchanted about that too. In his *Tale* he
describes the feverish work of floating timber downstream in spring,
and marvels that he was never ill, even though he laboured in icy water
from dawn to dusk. (As a boy in Viatka, he recalls, he had twice been
in hospital with rheumatic fever after a simple cold.) A few weeks later
he left Il'ia and sailed downriver by raft.

In the *Tale* there is no record of the months between Grin's return to Viatka from the Urals in August 1900, and the beginning of his stay in Sevastopol' in the summer of 1903. For what little information exists about this period, one must rely largely upon as yet unpublished sections of the memoirs of Grin's wives.

Returning from the Urals, he took a job as a bath-house attendant at the station of Murashi, sixty versts from Viatka, and then in April 1901, left for the Kotlas area to the north, aiming to live in the forests as a trapper. But he returned home after only a week and then worked for a few months on a barge, sailing the Viatka, Kama and Volga rivers, a period reflected in his unfinished tale *Prison Days of Yore (Tiuremnaia starina)* (1933).[52] For much of 1901, however, he appears to have lived in Viatka, probably largely at his father's expense, and to have drifted casually in his usual fashion from job to job.

Finally, encouraged by his father who was dismayed at his son's shiftlessness, Grinevskii volunteered for the army. He was sent via Cheliabinsk to Penza, and on 18 March 1902, enlisted in the 213th Orovaiskii reserve infantry battalion there as a private. But as might be expected, he disliked army life intensely and proved a poor soldier. "My army service was spent in constant and violent revolt against coercion," he recalled later. "My father's dreams that army discipline would make a man of me did not come true."[53] His only consolation was that for once, at least, he was clothed and well-fed. On 8 July 1902, he deserted, but night-blindness hampered his escape and he was captured on the 17th.[54] It is not known where he spent those nine days, and until the tale *The Detention Tent (Arestnaia palatka)*—believed to refer to this episode—is found, they must remain a mystery.

It was in Penza that Grinevskii first associated with the Socialist Revolutionary (SR) Party and, as he reveals in *Prison Days of Yore*, attended secret meetings held by the local cell and read revolutionary works. Perhaps it was no coincidence that during his period of desertion a revolutionary leaflet was found outside the camp.[55] According to Nina Grin, it was Aleksandr Studentsov, one of the Penza SR's, who suggested that Grinevskii scatter leaflets and proclamations in the barrack square.[56] Though Grin himself undoubtedly exaggerates when he writes in *Prison Days* that he scattered "a thousand"[57] leaflets, his revolutionary fervour is unquestionable. Nina Grin puts it thus: ". . . he was astounded by this new, strange, hitherto unseen and unsuspected world of struggle against coercion that had opened up before him. To him—a man already so very painfully pounded by life—hatred for the existing regime was especially understandable."[58] The Penza SR's, and in particular Student-sov, enabled Grinevskii to desert finally from the army on 28 November 1902. The SR period of his life was to last for the next four years, and it was to be the SR movement that discovered his talent as a writer.

The first seven months of this period, from December 1902, until July 1903, are a blank in Grin's biography, and only others' records or his own stories provide any guide. According to his first wife, Vera Pavlovna, Grin went first to Simbirsk and then to Nizhnii Novgorod. Selected to undertake terrorist activity for the SR's, in the summer of 1903 he was sent into "quarantine" at Tver' for about two weeks, so that it would become clear whether he was being watched by the police.[59] His subsequent refusal to carry out the terrorist act planned for him is illustrated by the story *Quarantine (Karantin)* (1907).[60] He was then sent as a propagandist to Saratov and Tambov, where he met the SR regional leader, Naum Iakovlevich Bykhovskii.[61] From Tambov the two men travelled together to Ekaterinoslav, and in August 1903, to Kiev. After a month's propaganda work there, Grin was sent first to Odessa and then to Sevastopol'.

Vera Pavlovna writes that the head of the Saratov SR group, a certain Starinkievich, later proved to be a traitor, and she therefore believes that Grin's story about an *agent provocateur, Night (Noch')* (1907), is based on fact.[62] Similarly, other tales of Grin's SR cycle, such as *Marat* (1907),[63] and *The Little Committee (Malen'kii komitet)* (1908),[64] are also drawn from his personal experience. In his *Autobiographical Tale* he reveals the inadequacies of the small SR group in Sevastopol'. Of one of its members he writes: "The teacher was a gas-bag, had done nothing of a revolutionary nature, and just frightened the other members of the organisation by proclaiming loudly on the street whenever he met them: 'We must throw a bomb!' or: 'When are we going to hang all these scoundrels?'"[65]

It was Bykhovskii who first detected Grinevskii's literary talent when the latter was writing SR proclamations at his request, and suggested to him: ". . . it seems to me that you could become a writer."[66] Many years later Grin was to recall the boundless significance of that trivial remark: "It was like a revelation, like the sweeping tornado of first love. I began to tremble at these words, realising that this was the sole thing which would make me happy, the sole thing for which, evidently without knowing it, my being had been yearning since childhood. . . . the seed had fallen into my soul and begun to grow. I had found my place in life."[67]

Eventually Grinevskii's agitation in Sevastopol' attracted the attention of the police, and on 11 November 1903, he was arrested for propaganda among both sailors of the Black Sea Fleet and artillerymen of the shore batteries. More than ninety other suspects were arrested at the same time. A search of Grinevskii's room revealed twenty-eight brochures of revolutionary content, among them pieces such as *The Herald of the Russian Revolution (Vestnik k russkoi revoliutsii)*, *The Terrorist Element in our Programme (Terroristicheskii element v nashei programme)* and *The Struggle of the Rostov Workers against the Tsarist Government (Bor'ba rostovskikh rabochikh s tsarskim pravitel'stvom)*.[68] Living on a false passport as Aleksandr Stepanovich Grigor'ev, Grinevskii when interrogated did not reveal his real name until 22 December 1903[69] (and not straightaway as he implies in his *Tale*[70]), at which point it became clear that he was a soldier who had deserted. He was then imprisoned in Sevastopol' gaol. The impression he made upon his interrogators was that he was a man of "reserved temperament, embittered and capable of anything, even of risking his life."[71]

A rescue attempt organised by fellow-SR's on 17 December failed, and Grinevskii's case dragged on while he languished in gaol. Whilst in prison he encouraged another inmate, N. N. Nikandrov, to write down for publication the amusing anecdotes which the latter would shout from his window to those exercising in the yard below. In his unpublished reminiscences of Grin, Nikandrov states that the paper *Krymskii vestnik* ("The Crimean Herald"), with which Grinevskii was apparently connected, later published some of these tales.[72]

A request made by Grinevskii in May 1904, to the minister of the interior for a transfer of his case to Viatka, brought no response. As a soldier he was to be tried by a military court for desertion, and the SR's engaged the progressive lawyer, A. S. Zarudnyi, to defend him. Finally, on 22 February 1905, the case was heard and the prosecutor asked for twenty years' hard labour. But Zarudnyi's speech for the defence was outstanding and Grinevskii was sentenced instead to ten years' exile in Siberia. He was kept in prison for another six months, however, until the sentence was confirmed in late August. But a second trial now awaited him. Investigation into revolutionary propaganda carried out among working people (who were not members of the armed forces), had involved him in a mass trial of Social Democrats (SD's) in Feodosia, and he was tried there with them. This time he was sentenced to a year's imprisonment, the term to run concurrently with the earlier one of exile. An attempt to organise his escape from Feodosia prison was unsuccessful and Grinevskii was soon transferred to Sevastopol' gaol. He was eventually released under the political amnesty of 21 October 1905, before his sentence of exile had been put into effect.

A month after his release from prison, the SR organisation sent Grinevskii to Petersburg at his own request. Perhaps before leaving Sevastopol' he witnessed the shelling of the mutinous cruiser *Ochakov* by the shore batteries on 15 November 1905, and in this memorable and tragic event found the inspiration for his story about the leader of the mutiny, *The Tale of Lieutenant Schmidt (Povest' o leitenante Shmidte)*.[73] Sandler believes that Grin went to Petersburg to see his fellow-SR, Ekaterina Bibergal' (whom he had fallen in love with while in Sevastopol'), who had escaped to Switzerland from exile in Archangel Province and then secretly returned to the capital.[74] However, she appears to have realised that Grinevskii's faith in the SR cause was not as complete as her own, but when she refused to marry him, he drew a pistol and shot her in the left side. Fortunately the wound was not severe and after surgery she quickly recovered. As might be expected, despite all Grinevskii's attempts to make amends, their relationship rapidly came to an end.[75]

On 7 January 1906, during the liquidation by police of the terrorist "Fighting Wing" *(boevoi letuchii otriad)* of the SR's in Petersburg, Grinevskii was arrested under the false name of Nikolai Ivanovich Mal'tsev.[76] He appears to have been detained by chance, simply because he happened to be within the area of the police swoop at the time. Presumably he had resorted to living on a false passport so as to avoid being exiled without trial—a fate which befell many former prisoners freed under the amnesty of the previous autumn. After his arrest he was imprisoned in the Kresty (Vyborg Side) gaol in Petersburg, and was often visited by Natalia, his adoptive sister.

Grin's future first wife, Vera Pavlovna Abramova (1882-1951), then twenty-four and working in the Political Red Cross organisation for the help of political prisoners and exiles, first met him when she visited him in the Kresty gaol in the spring of 1906. She did this as a fictitious fiancée, a device then frequently employed to gain access to prisoners. Two years younger than Grinevskii, she was the highly educated daughter of a prominent civil servant and was of German descent on her mother's side. Later she was to write several tales for children which were published in various journals, among them *Vskhody* ("Corn-Shoots"), *Chto i kak chitat' detiam* ("What and How to Read to Children"), and *Tropinka* ("The Path").[77] While Grinevskii was in prison they corresponded and she visited him regularly.

2. Contributors to the *Shipovnik* ("Sweetbriar") almanacs, 1909. Standing, left to right: N. Oliger, P. Potëmkin, A. Kotylev, A. S. Grin. Seated: L. Andruson, M. Artsybashev, N. Bashkin, V. Lenskii, Ia. Godin. (A gift from a private collection.)

3. Aleksandr Grin, Sevastopol', 1923. (A gift from a private collection.)

4. Aleksandr Grin in 1926. (A gift from a private collection.)

5. Aleksandr Grin in 1928. (A gift from a private collection.)

In April 1906, Grinevskii was sentenced to four years' exile in To-
bolsk Province, the term to begin from 29 March of the same year. On
the way there, in Tiumen', he met his former SR leader, Bykhovskii,
who gave him money and a false passport. Reaching Turinsk, their assigned place of residence, Grinevskii and some fellow-exiles plied their
guards with drink and on 11 June 1906, escaped, travelling sixty versts
by cart to the nearest railway station. Via Samara and Saratov, helped
by fellow-SR's, Grinevskii eventually reached Moscow, where Bykhovskii urged him to write a propaganda story *(agitka)* for distribution a-
mongst soldiers. This was to be Grin's first tale, *Private Panteleev's Service (Zasluga riadovogo Panteleeva)* (1906).[78] Though both its editor
and typesetter were arrested and the work confiscated, Grin avoided arrest as the pamphlet was unsigned and those accused did not reveal his
name.

Vera Pavlovna must have been the main reason for Grin's rapid return
to Petersburg, for soon after his departure for exile he had written to
her the significant words: "I want you to become everything for me:
mother, sister and wife."[79] His tale *A Hundred Versts Down the River
(Sto vërst po reke)* (1912),[80] reproduces many of the circumstances of
his escape and reflects his attachment for Vera Pavlovna. Since the passport he had was unreliable, after a month in Petersburg he travelled to
Viatka, where his father, by then accountant in the local hospital, pro-
cured for him the passport of a certain Aleksei Alekseevich Mal'ginov,
recently deceased.

During these first months in Petersburg Grin wrote a second *agitka,
The Elephant and the Pug-Dog (Slon i mos'ka)* (1906),[81] which, like
the first, was confiscated by the police while still at the printer's. In late
September or early October he wrote a third tale, *To Italy (V Italiiu)*,[82]
which was published in the evening edition of the Petersburg paper *Birzhevye vedomosti* ("The Stock-Exchange Gazette"), for 5 December
1906. This was his first "legal" work and was signed with the cryptonym
A. A. ––––v. Early in 1907, when requested by Izmailov, editor of the
above paper, to choose a pseudonym if he did not wish to reveal his real
name, Grin first used what was to become his accustomed signature of
"A. S. Grin," under his tale *Chance (Sluchai)* in the 25 March issue of
the newspaper *Tovarishch* ("Comrade").[83]

Vera Pavlovna's father strongly disapproved of his daughter's liaison
because he saw Grin as having neither education nor future. Nevertheless, in the autumn of 1907 she began to live with Grin on Vasil'evskii
Island, though the couple were as yet unable to marry because of Grin's

illegal status. In the summer of 1907 Vera's father had taken a *dacha* at Ozerki near Petersburg, and the first anniversary of the couple's unofficial marriage the following year is reflected in Grin's tale *The Dacha by the Big Lake (Dacha bol'shogo ozera)* (1909).[84] In it relations between husband and wife are far from happy. The stress often caused by differences in temperament between Grin and Vera Pavlovna was heightened by the couple's constant material difficulties. Grin's literary output in these early years was not large. In 1907, for example, he had fewer than ten tales published, among them *Chance, Oranges (Apel'siny)*,[85] *At Leisure (Na dosuge)*,[86] and *The Beloved (Liubimyi)*.[87] Vera Pavlovna's work in the laboratory of the Geological Institute provided a more regular income, but in general the couple had very little money and were often forced to resort to the pawnbroker.

As for Grin's revolutionary activities, Nina Grin writes that after his return from Turinsk to Petersburg, he left the SR's altogether: "Work for the [SR] party had not satisfied him for a long time now; for him it was the spring-board from which he sprang into literature and which enabled him to understand and find himself. But from now on his path lay in a different direction . . . he was engrossed in his literary work. He had found himself at last."[88] Vera Pavlovna recalls that Grin now said of his activity for the SR's: "I don't want to work any more, I'm tired, I don't want to take any risks."[89] But whatever his private feelings about the SR movement at this time, he still appeared to take a definite pro-SR stand in several tales. This is illustrated, for example, by the fact that in July 1907, the sixth number of the journal *Trudovoi put'* ("The Working Way"), containing Grin's story *Night*,[90] was confiscated by the Petersburg censorship committee. Referring to *Night*, the censor wrote: "The characters in it are members of one of the provincial committees of the SR party, and the theme of the work is the murder of political agents by the SR's. . . . the story is told in such a way that there can be no doubt of the author's intention to portray the revolutionaries and murderers as men of irreproachable integrity and lofty heroism, but the police agents as cowards and villains altogether deserving of the fate which befalls them."[91]

All Grin's tales of 1906 and 1907 were published early in February 1908, by Kotel'nikov, an acquaintance, in a first volume of ten collected stories entitled *The Magic Cap (Shapka nevidimka)*, and bearing the sub-title *Tales of Revolutionaries (Rasskazy o revoliutsionerakh)*.[92] The unusual title of the collection was devised by Vera Pavlovna: it conveyed to her the secret manner of their life together, with Grin concealing his identity by living under an assumed name and writing under a pseudo-nym. He was apparently dissatisfied with the book, however, feeling that between the time of writing and its publication his work had improved considerably. The story *Night*, confiscated the previous year by the censor, reappeared in the collection as *The Underground (Podzemnoe)*.

During these years Grin began to move in Bohemian circles in the capital and made the acquaintance of many Petersburg *littérateurs*, among them the critic Pil'skii, the poets Leonid Andruson, Apollon Korinfskii and Iakov Godin, and the authors A. I. Kuprin, L. N. Andreev and A. Chapygin. As Vera Pavlovna recalls sadly, he also began to drink and to disappear for a day or more at a time.

At the end of 1908 Grin wrote the exotic story *Reno Island (Ostrov Reno)*,[93] which he personally considered his first work of true literary merit and the turning-point in his career as a writer. "This is my road,"[94] was his comment upon finishing it. It was published in number six of the monthly *Novyi zhurnal dlia vsekh* ("The New Journal for All") for 1909, and afterwards Grin always referred to its editor, V. S. Miroliubov, as his literary godfather.

In the spring of 1909,[95] on the advice of the journalist V. A. Posse, and still using the false name of A. A. Mal'ginov, Grin wrote to Maxim Gorky on Capri, asking tentatively for Gorky's opinion of his work and enquiring as to whether a collection of his, Grin's, stories might be published by Gorky's *Znanie* ("Knowledge") organisation (see Appendix A). Gorky's reply—if indeed there was one—has never been found.

Highly significant for Grin's literary development because of the appearance of *Reno Island*, the year 1909 also saw the publication of his deeply pessimistic story *Paradise (Rai)*,[96] in which the despondent mood of the years of political reaction after 1905 finds a sombre reflection. The following year a second collection of his work appeared, published by the *Zemlia* ("Land") publishing house, and containing both stories inspired by his SR experiences, such as *The Little Committee* and *The Telegraphist from Mediansky Pine Forest (Telegrafist iz medianskogo bora)* (1908),[97] together with newer ones, such as *Reno Island* and *The Lanfier Colony (Koloniia Lanfier)* (1910),[98] which heralded his literary maturity. A collection of tales by Skitalets, Potapenko, Barantsevich and others, entitled *A Book of Stories (Kniga rasskazov)*, and published in the same year, 1910, included Grin's *Khons's Estate (Imenie Khonsa)*,[99] *The River (Reka)*,[100] *Arventur*,[101] *The Evening (Vecher)*[102] and *Silver of the South (Serebro iuga)*.[103] Literary critics, notably A. G. Gornfel'd of the prestigious journal *Russkoe bogatstvo* ("Russian Wealth"), now forecast a bright future for the budding author.[104]

In July 1910, Grin spent about three weeks working as a waiter in a leper colony in Iamburg (now Kingisepp) west of Petersburg, where the brother of his friend Andruson was a doctor. (Later he related his impressions of this stay to Aleksandr Kuprin, who was utterly fascinated by his account.[105]) When he returned from this visit, on the morning of 27 July 1910, Grin was arrested for living on a false passport, and the fact that he was an escaped exile soon came to light. Later it became clear that he had been betrayed by a literary acquaintance, A. I. Kotylev, to whom Grin had revealed his real name during a drunken argument. Vera Pavlovna was away in Kislovodsk at the time and only learnt of his arrest several days later.

Meanwhile Grin was interrogated and immediately given a three-month prison sentence for using a false passport. He quickly requested permission to marry, and then wrote two petitions, one to the tsar and the other to the minister of the interior, asking for clemency and the peace and quiet necessary for literary work. Though during the previous four years in Petersburg he may have been visited by people associated with the SR movement, there is no evidence to suggest that he himself had engaged in any further revolutionary activity. In the second petition, of 1 August 1910, he spoke of the radical change that had taken place in his political views. "During the past five years I have done nothing which would confer the right to treat me as an enemy of the State. . . . there has been a complete volte-face in my outlook which has made me strictly and categorically avoid all contact with political groups."[106] Referring to his literary work, he added that his writings were essentially artistic, contained only general psychological concepts and symbols, and were "devoid of any political tendencies whatsoever."[107] The years of hard living and uncertainty were evidently beginning to tell on his priorities. "My constitution is in ruins," he wrote, "and my sole desire is to live a quiet, family life, working to the best of my ability in the field of Russian literature."[108]

The apologetic tone of both petitions was a far cry from his stubborn refusal to ask for clemency when jailed in Sevastopol' in 1903,[109] and may well have been feigned. Alternatively, he may have written the petitions while suffering from depression and loneliness or, as Sandler suggests,[110] at the instigation of Vera Pavlovna. Nevertheless, it seems clear from them that he had by now chosen his role in life—that of writer—and was prepared to sacrifice a great deal in order to preserve it. Despite his petitions, however, he was sentenced to two years' exile in Archangel Province.

After much difficulty Grin and Vera Pavlovna were married in the prison church on 24 October 1910,[111] and on 31 October they left by train for Archangel, Grin travelling under guard and Vera Pavlovna accompanying him voluntarily in a separate carriage.

Their life together in Petersburg had been far from easy. What little money Grin had earned by writing he had spent rashly, often on drink, and for this reason Vera Pavlovna had even left him for a few months in 1908. Grin longed for domestic comfort and peace, yet at the same time was reluctant to sacrifice the independence to which he had grown so accustomed during his wandering youth. Drink and the Bohemian circles of Petersburg were part of that independence, and his involvement in the city's riotous life was eventually to prove largely responsible for the breakdown of his marriage with Vera Pavlovna. However, the following two years of exile in Archangel Province were to be a brief lull in the progressive deterioration of their relationship. Away from the demoralising influence of Petersburg's Bohemia, Grin drank very little and became, if only temporarily, a changed person.

CHAPTER II

ARCHANGEL, PETERSBURG AND PETROGRAD
1910-1921
EXILE AND BOHEMIAN

On the way to Archangel, Grin was held for two days in the transit prison of Vologda. Then on 8 November 1910, Vera Pavlovna and he left Archangel by sledge for Pinega, about 120 kilometres to the east, after a petition from Grin requesting permission to remain in Archangel itself had been refused. Four days' journey brought them to Pinega, their assigned place of residence, of which the population of about 2,000 included some 200 political exiles. It is thought that a woman relative of Grin's, a certain Antonina, was already living there, but it is highly unlikely that she was one of his sisters, as I. V. Myl'tsina claims.[1] Among the exiles in Pinega was Nikolai Studentsov, the son of a Penza priest, whose brother Aleksandr had helped Grin to desert from the army there. As Vera Pavlovna's father sent his daughter 75 roubles per month and as Grin received the monthly state subsidy customarily given to political exiles, the couple lived quite comfortably in Pinega.

During his first months in exile Grin rested, wrote, read a great deal, and according to at least one fellow-exile,[2] hardly drank at all. But with the advent of spring, 1911, he became irritable and bored. He began to hunt and fish, however, finding immense enjoyment in the beauty of the wild forests and countless lakes around Pinega, an enjoyment reflected later in such tales as *A Hundred Versts Down the River* and *The Mysterious Forest (Tainstvennyi les)* (1913).[3] The description in the latter of a hunter's unsuccessful pursuit of a visionary golden cockerel is drawn directly from Grin's experience in the forests around Pinega. The incident was important for, as Nina Grin recalls, it brought about a radical change in his whole attitude to hunting. "The intelligence, suffering and terror of the bird left a painful impression upon Aleksandr Stepanovich's imagination, and in his soul he turned away from hunting as an entertainment. In his mature years he accepted hunting only as a necessity, a means of subsistence, . . . and was not attracted to it as he had been in his younger days."[4]

It is interesting to note that when a large group of new exiles arrived in Pinega early in the spring of 1911—they were students exiled for their part in demonstrations connected with the funeral of Tolstoy in November 1910—Grin did not become particularly friendly with any of them. As O. Voronova suggests,[5] perhaps this was because he saw in them only the transient revolutionary ardour of dilettantes. At the end of June, Grin's younger brother Boris, then fifteen years old, came to visit him. Earlier in the year, maintaining that he had a heart condition and was generally weak, Grin had asked to be transferred to Archangel, where he would have better access to medical treatment. In the late summer of 1911 he was granted permission to move from Pinega to Këgostrov in the Dvina delta, only three kilometres from Archangel itself. In late August 1911, he travelled by steamer along the rivers Pinega and Northern Dvina to Archangel, a journey which, according to Vera Pavlovna, provided him with much material for the tale *A Hundred Versts Down the River*. While in Këgostrov he wrote the stories *The Blue Cascade of Telluri (Sinii kaskad Telluri)*[6] and *Kseniia Turpanova* (1912).[7] Vera Pavlovna claims that both works contain autobiographical details, and that the latter is evidence of Grin's unfaithfulness to her,[8] but this is refuted by the reminiscences of other exiles.[9] The second tale does, however, give a realistic picture of the gloomy surroundings of Këgostrov and their demoralising effect upon the exiles.

An attempt in November and December 1911, to secure Grin's early release—both his wife and his father petitioned the minister of the interior—proved unsuccessful. His term of exile was due to end on 15 May 1912, and in March of that year his request to spend the remaining two months of his sentence in Archangel itself was granted. On 21 March he and Vera Pavlovna moved into the town and in late April she went to Petersburg to prepare for their return. On 16 May Grin finally reached the capital. Later he often declared that the months of exile in the far north were the very best in their few years together.

Once back in Petersburg, he soon plunged into familiar Bohemian circles again. This time, however, he began to drink even more than before. Vera Pavlovna writes that their relations are described in Grin's story *Hell Regained (Vozvrashchënnyi ad)* (1915),[10] in which the journalist, Mark, becomes completely indifferent to Vizi, his fiancée. Quoting from that story, Vera Pavlovna comments bitterly that in reality everything was far worse: "Without any doubt Aleksandr

Stepanovich was leading us towards a separation. The romance had gone from our relationship, and I understood to the full the two-sided, rather frightening essence of his character."[11] Though life together in the autumn of 1912 was still tolerable, she writes, even that consolation disappeared with Grin's increasing absences and bouts of drunkenness. On the rare occasions when he was at home, he was "gloomy and openly indifferent"[12] towards her, and she felt quite unwanted.

Eventually, in the spring of 1913, the break came, when Grin returned home in a vile mood after an absence of two days. "He insulted me in a most coarse manner," Vera Pavlovna writes, "and the thought that something similar could happen again was intolerable to me. I had to go."[13] And go she did, leaving a letter perhaps resembling that left by Vizi for Mark in *Hell Regained*,[14] and giving no address. But Grin traced her and they were briefly reconciled. She agreed to live with him for three months that summer, and provided he did not drink, she promised to return to him permanently. But if he persisted in his present behaviour, she said, there would be a final separation. After only a fortnight, however, Grin began to drink heavily again, and she realised that her "role in Aleksandr Stepanovich's life was finished."[15]

In her memoirs Vera Pavlovna gives her own explanation as to why their marriage broke up:

> "For the first six years, our life together was sustained by his capacity for great and genuine tenderness. . . . Grin was an escaped exile, living illegally on a false passport. During that time we became close to one another. He had no source of income, no occupation and no influential acquaintances. At the time he needed a loving person who would share with him both sadness and joy. But by 1913 his position was completely different: he had a legal passport and was threatened by neither arrest nor exile; furthermore, during the previous seven years he had gained for himself the reputation of a talented writer. This gave him both income and status, as well as admirers of his talent. But I remained the ordinary girl from the intelligentsia [*intelligentka*] that I had been before—something that could no longer satisfy him."[16]

Nina Grin is probably nearer the mark, however, when she refers instead to a fundamental difference in ideals and background between

Grin and his first wife. Shortly before Grin's death many years later, she wrote to Vera Pavlovna:

"Aleksandr Stepanovich has always assured me that he had no wish to be divorced from you, but that there was between you a mutual failure to understand each other's ideals of life. . . . His ideal was always that he should be in charge, alone in all the world with his wife, sitting by the camp-fire ready to shelter her from the rain in bad weather; on the other hand, according to him your ideal at that time was the welfare of people in general, but not your own personal welfare. He was a vagrant by nature, with an undisciplined, unpolished, fiery character and a thirst for life, while you were a girl from the Petersburg intelligentsia with fixed habits and views, . . . and with notions about life but no real knowledge of it."[17]

Perhaps more important still is the fact that Vera Pavlovna lacked faith in her husband as a writer and seemed unable to appreciate the deeper significance of his work. Whilst liking the early revolutionary tales, which eventually dissatisfied Grin himself, she disapproved of the more typically Grinian *Reno Island* and *The Lanfier Colony*, and would say to him: "Why do you . . . write fantastic nonsense? You should write a big novel about everyday life [*bytovoi roman*], and then you'd become a well-known author straightaway."[18] Disappointed and misunderstood, Grin said later that Vera Pavlovna wanted him to write "as people do for the [popular] weekly supplement to the paper *Sovremennoe slovo* ("The Contemporary Word").[19]

Grin and his wife separated in the summer of 1913 and she refused his entreaties to join him again that autumn. For a year or more he visited her three or four times a week, then less frequently with the passage of time. Pathetic in his fear of loneliness, he begged her not to "abandon him to mankind."[20] Their divorce was only made official seven years later, in 1920, when Vera Pavlovna married Professor K. P. Kalitskii, an eminent geologist. From the time they parted in 1913 until Grin's death in 1932, however, relations between Vera Pavlovna and him remained friendly. She sent money to Grin and his second wife when they were almost penniless in the late 1920s, and gave them valuable help with a subsequent lawsuit against a Leningrad publisher.

As in the years of his early wanderings, so the details of Grin's life between his separation from Vera Pavlovna and his second marriage in 1921 are far from full. He left no record of this period, and one can only rely on the incomplete memoirs of both wives and on several shorter accounts by various friends and acquaintances, none of which provide any detailed information.

Vera Pavlovna's departure certainly caused Grin immense pain and distress. In a letter to Leonid Andreev at this time he wrote: "My existence at the moment is miserable. For a long time now—almost a week —I have done no work. And this is why: because of my behaviour (alcoholism) my wife has left me. (She was quite right to do so.) The nervous shock that I am experiencing has drawn me into debt, and, in the material sense, into temporary destitution."[21] The intense loneliness that began when Vera Pavlovna left him was to continue largely undiminished until he married again. We must assume that during the months after his wife's departure, Grin revelled and drank as before, but as Nina Grin puts it, "debauchery did not pacify his soul."[22] I. Sokolov-Mikitov, who knew him well during these years, recalls that he was not the kind of person who could look after himself properly in the material sense, being "generally speaking . . . a man badly equipped for everyday life."[23] To this period, too, belongs Grin's acquaintance with Larissa Reisner,[24] then a journalist and subsequently an active Bolshevik.

Unfortunately, not all Grin's difficulties at this time were of a marital kind. Because of his revolutionary past he was still under intermittent police surveillance, and after the outbreak of the First World War this was intensified and continued until the summer of 1915.[25] But drink was an infinitely more serious problem. Early in 1914, on the advice of Gleb Uspenskii's son who had himself benefitted from treatment there for drunkenness, Grin spent a month in the Petersburg nursing home run by the well-known psychologist, Dr. Troshin. After a three-day drinking bout with Kuprin, he had decided to stamp out his alcoholism with the help of Troshin's hypnosis and to turn over a new leaf. Writing to his journalist friend A. E. Roziner to ask for a loan, Grin said that he was ill "in a way that I hope you will *never* be ill."[26] Sincere though his desire was to mend his ways, the attempt came to nothing, and to Troshin's annoyance Grin soon discharged himself from the nursing home.

Despite his personal problems, however, Grin produced a relatively large volume of work in the years after his separation from Vera Pavlovna. But unfortunately his name was lost among those of more popular authors such as Kamenskii, Potapenko, Muizhel', Artsybashev, Lazarevskii, Avseenko, Iasinskii, Verbitskaia and others, the majority of whom are now forgotten. Thus the better, so-called "thick" (*tolstye*) journals rarely found room to publish his work. Yet, at a time when he was forced to write in order to live, and when excessively national-istic, anti-German stories were the only ones sure of publication, he still managed to preserve his literary integrity. A letter of this time to his friend V. S. Miroliubov, editor of *Novyi zhurnal dlia vsekh*, explains his attitude: "Things are difficult for me. Russian journals and critics recognise me only reluctantly and against their will; to them I am unfamiliar, alien and strange. Because of this—that is because of my constant struggle and fatigue—I often drink and very heavily at that. But since there is nothing greater for me in art (in literature) than art itself, I do not consider yielding to tendentious demands that are more cruel than the medieval inquisition. Otherwise there is no sense in working at one's beloved task. And so I call occasionally on you . . . to catch a breath of air untainted by scribblings and clannishness."[27] Like Miroliubov, Arkadii Averchenko, editor of the journal *Novyi satirikon* ("The New Satyricon"), was well-disposed towards Grin and liked his work. Feeling a protective affection for him, he tried to give Grin self-confidence as a writer, for he realised that the younger man often belittled his own talent. Grin went on contributing satirical poems and skits to *Novyi satirikon* until 1918.

1915 was probably the most productive year of Grin's career, for in it he wrote over a hundred fables, poems and tales. As in 1914, many were of a strongly chauvinistic and anti-German kind, in both humorous and serious vein. Satire, too, flowed abundantly from his pen during these years, finding its way into the cheaper papers and journals of the time. But much of it is of doubtful quality and, as Grin himself once suggested, is hardly representative of his true literary self: "I am not a satirist. I do not have a satirical attitude to life. . . ."[28] In many cases he was simply writing for money, and seems miraculously to have been able to keep separate the two parts of his writer's self: the bread-winner able to toss off in minutes an intriguing but mediocre tale, and the literary artist capable of unstinting effort to achieve the desired effect. 1916 was fruitful too. Grin contributed largely to the papers *Petrogradskii listok* ("The Petrograd News-Sheet") and *Birzhevye vedomosti*, and to the journals *Ogonëk* ("The Little Light") and *Gerkules* ("Hercules"), the latter being a sporting maga-zine. Among his best works of this year were the tales *The Black Diamond (Chërnyi almaz)*,[29] *Punishment (Nakazanie)*,[30] *Around the World (Vokrug sveta)*[31] and *The Labyrinth (Labirint)*.[32]

In late August or early September 1916, Grin once more attracted official disapproval when he was banished from Petrograd by the city governor for making disrespectful remarks about the tsar in a restaurant. He chose as his place of brief exile the station of Lunatiokki, some forty miles from the capital on the railway line to Finland, and did not return to Petrograd until after the February Revolution, on 22 February 1917. The story of his journey back to the capital—most of it made on foot—is told in the autobiographical sketch *On Foot to the Revolution (Peshkom na revoliutsiiu),*[33] first published in the summer of 1917. As Grin writes here: "The uncertainty of what was happening in Petrograd drew me to the capital with irresistible force."[34] Apart from this sketch, he seems to have written and said very little in a direct way about the February Revolution. Moreover, not a single letter by Grin dated 1917 has been found. From the perspective of the Soviet era Nina Grin writes that the "bourgeois" (February) revolution did not satisfy her husband, because he saw that in spite of it everything remained just the same in Russia.[35] However, as the above sketch suggests, he was not at all hostile to the first revolution, though at the same time he appears to have welcomed it as a romantic rather than a political event.

Among his almost non-existent baggage on his return journey to Petrograd was the manuscript of a tale entitled *Red Sails (Krasnye parusa),* later to become his famous *feeriia, Scarlet Sails (Alye parusa).* In July 1916, he had written his *Reflections on "Red Sails" (Razmyshleniia nad "Krasnymi parusami")*[36] after being tremendously impressed by a model yacht with scarlet sails that he had seen in a Nevskii Prospect toyshop. These *Reflections* were the basis of the eventual *Scarlet Sails,* his first novella.

The October Revolution seems to have made a much more profound impression on Grin than its predecessor in February. According to Nina Grin he was both frightened and elated by the events of October 1917, though she is perhaps guilty of exaggeration when she writes that "he was filled with joyful emotion, for he knew the seamy side of life as no one else did. For him the Revolution was the birth of justice, the happiness of those who until then had been beaten by life, those whose bodies and souls still ached from the pounding of life's fists."[37] Grin's attitude to the street violence of 1917 is illustrated by his short tales *Red Splashes of Blood (Krasnye bryzgi)*[38] and *The Corpses (Trupy),*[39] the newspaper cuttings of which are held by the Central State Archive of Literature and Art (TsGALI) in Moscow. Though both are undated, the pieces were almost certainly written shortly before the Bolshevik seizure of power, in the late autumn of 1917. Both works, and the second in particular, where the narrator (presumably Grin himself) visits a mortuary, are an indictment of violence and of public indifference to scenes of horror.

Grin wrote very little in 1918, and there is no evidence to suggest that his predilection for the bottle had diminished. Vera Pavlovna helped him in so far as she could during these difficult months. Among his few works of that year were the *étude Ears of Corn (Kolos'ia)*,[40] which conveys in stark terms the general hunger at the time; the biting satire on provincial prejudice, *Make a Grandmother! (Sdelaite babushku!)*[41]; and the amusing short story *Erna*,[42] published in the ephemeral paper *Vsevidiashchee oko* ("The All-Seeing Eye"), a delightful piece that displays yet again Grin's capacity for making the most of a trifling incident.

In the autumn of 1918 Grin informed Vera Pavlovna that he was married again, but the attachment was short-lived, for by the winter she heard that he was living alone once more. This brief liaison was apparently not with Maria Sergeevna Alonkina, as Sandler suggests,[43] but with Maria Vladislavovna Dolidze, an old acquaintance of Aleksandr Kuprin's. It lasted only three months and was almost certainly not an official marriage.[44]

As Grin rarely spoke of his past and usually destroyed his correspondence, it is very difficult to trace his friends and acquaintances in the years between his separation from Vera Pavlovna in 1913 and his second marriage in 1921. Of those friends who are known, Aleksandr Ivanovich Kuprin probably most deserves mention. It is not certain when he and Grin first met—it may well have been when Grin was in the Crimea in the early 1900s. But Grin undoubtedly knew him during the four years, 1906 to 1910, that he spent living on a false passport in Petersburg, and on his return from exile in Archangel Province in 1912 he fell in with him again. Grin once said that ideally he would have liked to begin his autobiographical record with what he called his "Kuprin time" (*"kuprinskoe vremia"*)—the Bohemian days of 1912 to 1914—and added mysteriously: *"there* is something worth recalling and writing about."[45]

Grin later acknowledged the immense encouragement given him by Kuprin, who was ten years his senior: "He gave me a great deal of help when I was beginning to write, during our frequent conversations at table."[46] It was Kuprin who suggested that Grin write a play and dedicate it to him, but Grin dedicated his verse tale *Li*[47] to him instead. The friendship between them was close and affectionate. "He was so dear to my heart," said Grin many years later, "that . . . even if he had written badly, it would have seemed to me that he wrote well."[48] Despite Kuprin's frequent vulgarity and his envy for others' literary success, Grin felt that in him "there sat a kindly artist." For his part, Kuprin liked Grin for what he called the younger man's "golden talent" and for his indifference to literary fame, something without which, he confessed, he himself could not survive. Kuprin's constant desire to excel in everything and be the focus of general attention was well known to Grin, and he recalled Kuprin's jealousy when he heard of the weeks Grin had spent in the leper colony in 1910, for that was an exploit of which he had never thought. Kuprin found it very hard to praise any other writer, Grin explained to his wife years later, so the affection and interest he had for the younger man and his work were very rare. Grin felt that he was the only author who did not arouse in Kuprin his "base feeling" of hostile rivalry, and for this reason, he believed, he came to know Kuprin as he really was. The link between the two men appears to have been broken when Kuprin emigrated after the Revolution, and by the time he returned to the USSR from Paris in 1937, Grin was dead.

Of the many literary critics whom he knew, it was with Arkadii Georgievich Gornfel'd of *Russkoe bogatstvo* that Grin became most friendly. He once said that Gornfel'd was the sole cultured critic who had written "seriously and thoughtfully"[49] about his work. Gornfel'd was responsible for the first valuable review of Grin's work, published in *Russkoe bogatstvo* in 1910,[50] and seven years later he gave a second very perceptive appraisal of Grin's writing in the same journal.[51] Grin always said that the critic's first article had given him "hope in himself."[52] From 1921 until leaving Petrograd in 1924, Grin would often visit Gornfel'd to ask for his advice on literary matters. When Grin read the final draft of *Scarlet Sails* to him, Gornfel'd was profoundly impressed, saying that this was Grin's most powerful work so far.

From early 1919 onwards, Grin's biography again becomes somewhat easier to trace. In January of that year he moved to a room in a house taken over by a group of writers known as the "Union of Belle-lettrists" (*"Soiuz deiatelei khudozhestvennoi literatury"*), on the 11th Line of Vasil'evskii Island. Among the residents were V. Voinov and his family, Iu. Slëzkin, Dmitrii Tsenzor and his wife, and V. Muizhel', while Gorky, Sologub, Blok, Chukovskii and Shishkov were also linked with the group. Muizhel' edited the cultural section of the journal *Plamia* ("The Flame") and Tsenzor worked on the paper *Krasnyi baltiiskii flot* ("The Red Baltic Fleet"), while Grin himself found work on the cultural section of *Krasnyi militsioner* ("The Red Militiaman"), a journal published by the Petrograd police. The society occupying the house only lasted until mid-1919, however: its members soon went off to join new associations, such as the House of Writers (*Dom literatorov*), the House of Scholars (*Dom uchënykh*), and the House of Arts (*Dom iskusstv*).

1919 saw little that was new from Grin's pen—a mere handful of works, all published in the journal *Plamia* and nearly all of them poems or verse, such as *The Factory of the Thrush and the Lark (Fabrika drozda i zhavoronka)*,[53] *The Crystal Vase (Khrustal'naia vaza)*,[54] *The Sick Wolf (Bol'noi volk)*[55] and *Movement (Dvizhenie)*.[56]

In the summer of 1919, when he was almost forty, Grin was called up for service in the Red Army. In September his brigade moved from its quarters in the Novocherkasskie barracks in Petrograd to the Belorussian town of Vitebsk, where he was detailed to work in a porcelain factory. Then he was transferred to Ostrov, south of Pskov and about two hundred miles south-west of the capital. Attached to a communications unit, he soon became exhausted by the strenuous work of laying telephone lines over deep snow, but though his condition was deteriorating rapidly, his requests for leave were refused. All the while, however, he carried in his kit-bag the manuscript of *Red Sails*, and though during all his months of service he never once looked at it, its presence sustained him. "Its closeness warmed my soul," he said later to Nina Grin, "for it was like an unbroken gossamer web linking me with the bright world of dreams."[57]

Eventually he became so depressed and weak that he felt he would rather be shot as a deserter than remain in the army any longer. His reading of Anna Vivanti's book *I Divoratori—Poglotiteli (The Devourers)*[58] in Russian translation—intensified his desire to leave the army rather than, as he put it, "drag out my tormenting existence in the rear, amid filth and cold."[59] Finally, in March 1920, tuberculosis was suspected and he was sent to Moscow by hospital train. Only three days after his departure, the White Poles wiped out his telephone brigade. Reaching Petrograd on 20 March, he stayed for a while with I. I. Karel', an acquaintance from his Këgostrov days. But weak and starving, he was soon very ill—so much so that he feared he might collapse and die on the street as many did at the time.

In desperation Grin went for help to Gorky, who gave him a note
for the city Commandant. In his turn the latter found him a bed in
the Smol'nyi infirmary. After three days there he was found to be
suffering from typhus. He thereupon wrote to Gorky, asking for a
loan of 3,000 roubles and for some honey—to enable him, as he said,
to sweat out the fever. He enclosed in his letter his will, by which, in
the event of his death, Vera Pavlovna, who was still his legal wife, was
to acquire exclusive rights over all his published and unpublished work
(see Appendix A). That same day, 26 April 1920, he was transferred to
the Botkin hospital where he spent a month. Here he received from
Gorky not only a letter but also the rare luxuries of white bread, butter
and honey. Afterwards he was to say to Nina Grin of this time: "Maxim
Gorky saved me, but for my inner self the stimulus for salvation came
from Anna Vivanti's *The Devourers*."[60] When discharged from hospital,
however, Grin was still extremely weak, and once more found himself
without food or accommodation. Again he roamed the starving city,
spending his nights with friends whenever they had room—a period reflected in his largely autobiographical tales *The Ratcatcher (Krysolov)*
(1924)[61] and *Fandango* (1927).[62]

In December 1919, with the help of Lenin, Gorky had organised in
Petrograd the Central Commission for the Improvement of Living
Conditions of Scholars *(Tsentral'naia komissiia po uluchsheniiu byta
uchënykh)* (TsKUBU).[63] One of the first institutions established
through Gorky's efforts was the House of Arts, to be followed in
January 1920, by the House of Scholars. The House of Arts was on the
corner of Nevskii Prospect and the Moika, in the former apartments
of the Eliseev brothers, owners of Russia's largest grocery business
before the Revolution but by now in emigration. Most of the House
was on the second floor, while the area beneath was occupied by the
empty premises of the former very large Crédit Lyonnais bank.[64]
The institution was first opened on 19 December 1919, with Gorky
at its head and the Commission for Popular Education *(Komissiia
narodnogo prosveshcheniia)* providing the funds. Very soon the House
included both hostel accommodation and a book counter *(knizhnyi
punkt)*. Needless to say, the demand for a place in this relatively
luxurious institution in a city stricken with hunger and cold was immense among artists, musicians and men of letters.

In the summer of 1920 Gorky arranged for Grin to be one of the
first writers assigned an "academic" food ration *(akademicheskii
paëk)*, and then found him a room in the House of Arts. He also put

6. Aleksandr Grin and Nina Nikolaevna Grin in the garden of their flat at 8 (now 10), Ulitsa Galereinaia, Feodosia, 1926. (IMLI, fond 95, opis' 1, No. 21.)

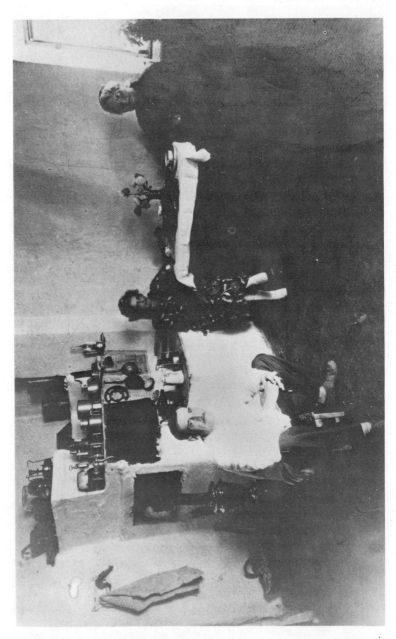

7. Aleksandr Grin, Nina Grin and her mother in the kitchen of their flat in Feodosia. Exact date unknown, but probably late 1920s. (A gift from a private collection.)

8. Nina Grin and her mother in the garden of 52 (now 56), Ulitsa K. Libknekhta, Staryi Krym, now the Grin *dom-muzei*. Exact date unknown, but probably early 1930s, possibly after Grin's death in 1932. (A gift from a private collection.)

Grin in touch with the publishing house of Z. I. Grzhebin and com-
missioned him to write two stories for young readers. The first concerned Stanley's search for Livingstone and later became *The Treasure
of the African Mountains (Sokrovishche afrikanskikh gor)* (1925),
appearing in abridged form as *Around the Central Lakes (Vokrug
tsentral'nykh ozër)* (1927).[65] The second, about Nansen's voyage on
the *Fram* to the North Pole, was entitled *The Mysterious Circle (Tainstvennyi krug)* but was also known as *Ice and Fire (Lëd i ogon')*. Both
were intended to be part of the series devised by Gorky and entitled
The Life of Remarkable People (Zhizn' zamechatel'nykh liudei). But
Grin's novella, *Scarlet Sails*, soon took precedence over them, and
though the first work was eventually published in 1925, *The Mysterious
Circle* was never completed. Several chapters of it survive, however,
with corrections made by Gorky on the manuscript.[66]

Among the inhabitants of the House of Arts were Mikhail Slonimskii, Vladimir Piast, Vsevolod Rozhdestvenskii, Osip Mandel'shtam,
Nadezhda Pavlovich, Olga Forsh, Viktor Shklovskii, Ilia Gruzdëv,
Nikolai Kliuev, Vladimir Pozner, Marietta Shaginian, Konstantin Fedin,
Lev Lunts, Nikolai Nikitin, Veniamin Kaverin, Nikolai Tikhonov
and Mikhail Zoshchenko. They were joined later by Vsevolod Ivanov
on his arrival from Siberia. (Many of these writers are described under
pseudonyms by Olga Forsh in her book about the House entitled *The
Mad Ship* [*Sumasshedshii korabl'*, 1931].[67]) In his reminiscences of
the House of Arts Vladislav Khodasevich remembers Grin at this time.
"An author of adventure stories," his description runs, "a gloomy,
tubercular man, who engaged in an everlasting and hopeless struggle
with the bosses of *Disk* [the nickname for *Dom iskusstv*], who struck
up acquaintance with practically no one, and who, so people said,
spent his time training cockroaches."[68] Despite apparent friction with
its administrators, Grin does not seem to have disliked his stay in the
House. His months there brought an improvement in his health, and
when Vera Pavlovna visited him in June 1920, she could see that the
enforced regime of sobriety in the institution was having a beneficial
effect on him.

With the House of Scholars and the House of Writers, the House of
Arts rapidly became one of the three foci of Petrograd's cultural
activity which came to the fore with astonishing vigour in the months
after the Revolution. Paradoxically, far from reducing this upsurge,
the severe privations in the city seem to have heightened it. The House
became the venue for highly varied lectures, discussions, musical eve-

nings, and prose and verse readings, and among its regular speakers numbered Belyi, Maiakovskii, Zamiatin and the Serapion Brethren. Filled with a stimulating atmosphere of creativity, the institution attracted people from all over Petrograd. Together with the material support it provided, Grin's new environment enabled him to begin work with a fresh sense of purpose.

His links with Gorky remained, and in July 1920, he wrote to him again, this time on Vera Pavlovna's behalf, asking if she might be given some biographical work for the Grzhebin publishing house (see Appendix A). Though many Soviet critics—notably N. P. Izergina[69]—tend to exaggerate both the role played by Gorky in Grin's career and their affection for one another, there is no doubt that they were firm, if not close, friends, and that to the end of his life Grin was profoundly grateful for Gorky's help when he was ill and starving in Petrograd. As he confessed to Nina Grin years later, when first in the House of Arts he was often moved to tears of gratitude for Gorky's help in finding him accommodation and food. But Gorky assisted Grin in the literary sense too. Exactly to what extent he did so is difficult to judge, as all the information available is of a very general nature. As stated above, however, it is certain that Gorky corrected the manuscript of Grin's unfinished tale *The Mysterious Circle*, for which Grin expressed his thanks. "I love to find your notes on my manuscript," he wrote to Gorky on 29 July 1920, "for in them I see and value your attention of which I am completely undeserving" (see Appendix A).

However, the two biographical stories requested by Gorky were shelved so that Grin could complete his first novella, *Scarlet Sails*. He had been working on the manuscript of it intermittently for almost five years now. As far as is known, he published nothing in 1920, and presumably worked on the novella for most of that year. On 4 December he read the first completed draft of it to Mikhail Slonimskii and on 8 December read it again to a gathering of members of the House of Arts. Well received, it was finally finished in April 1921, but not published until 1923.[70]

September 1920 saw the second visit made by H. G. Wells to Russia. At a banquet held in the Englishman's honour in the House of Writers, Grin made a speech which indicated his attitude towards his own work. Recalling Wells' story *Aepyornis Island*, in which from the egg of an unknown bird a castaway hatches a giant creature that attempts to kill him, Grin drew two analogies. In the man who hatched the extraordinary bird he saw the creative artist, and in the bird which then tried to kill him he saw the product of artistic imagination, the writer's dream. To Grin that dream was capable of destroying its creator. Though ostensibly speaking of Wells, Grin was clearly referring to himself. At about this time he jotted down in a notebook what was perhaps an idea for a story that seems never to have materialized: "Convicts of the imagination. Writers in the guise of inmates of a convict prison, dragging the burdens of their creative work."[71] According to Slonimskii, Grin's speech at the banquet was a re-affirmation of the literary views he had held before the Revolution, since it defended the position of the artist who chooses to be "left alone with his dream."[72]

Grin's relationships with women since his separation from Vera Pavlovna had not been serious, with the possible exception of his liaison with Maria Dolidze. But at the beginning of winter, 1918, he met his future second wife, then working in the office of the newspaper *Petrogradskoe ekho* ("The Petrograd Echo"), in which his poem *Daybreak (Zaria)* had been published on 26 January of that year. Like him, Nina Nikolaevna Koroshkova (*née* Mironova) (1894-1970) had been married before. Had she heeded the warnings of her friends about Grin, she might never have married him at all: ". . . beware of him, he's a dangerous man and he's done hard labour for the murder of his wife. . . . his past is very shady, and they say that when he was a sailor he killed an English captain somewhere off Africa and stole his trunk containing manuscripts. He knows English but carefully conceals the fact, and is gradually publishing the manuscripts as his own. . . ."[73] Such were the legends that had grown up around Grin's name, fostered by his taciturn nature, his exotic writing and his chequered youth. In a diluted form, some of them persist today.

Grin met Nina Nikolaevna again on 22 February 1921,[74] and they were married early in May. He was then forty and she twenty-six. Some two months before his marriage Grin received a letter from the committee of the House of Arts, signed by Gorky and Zamiatin, giving him a month to vacate his room there because of his repeated "foul oaths"[75] to officials of that institution (see Appendix B).

His second marriage proved a watershed in Grin's career. During the more settled years that it brought he was to consolidate his reputation with five novels and dozens of tales. In the years preceding this marriage he was, as Nina Grin puts it, "filled with themes, plots, characters and words, and could write a great deal frequently."[76] Now, however, he became less mercurial in his behaviour and steadier in his working habits: ". . . in him there was no longer conflagration, crackling and suddenness.

The flame of creativity burned powerfully, steadily and calmly."[77] Throughout the years to come, Nina Nikolaevna was to be an encouraging and guiding influence, for the alcoholism that had taken root in Bohemian Petersburg never lost its hold on him. In the long years of financial difficulty and privation that were to follow, she showed a capacity for self-sacrifice and understanding which Vera Pavlovna may never have possessed. At Nina's instigation Grin began to collect and keep all the work he published, something he had never done in earlier years, when so much material was lost and when he would say carelessly: "It's been printed—so whoever needs it will find it."[78] Nina Grin was also responsible for collecting much memoir material about her husband discovered since his death and for tracing several tales long considered lost during his lifetime. Her personal record of his life is the most valuable single document for the biographer.

CHAPTER III

THE LAST YEARS
1921-1932
MIGRANT AND NOVELIST

From June till mid-September 1921—their first summer together—
the Grins rented a room in a *dacha* at Toksovo, about forty kilometres
from Petrograd near the Finnish border. Here Grin made rough drafts
of his projected novel *Algol'—The Double Star (Algol'—zvezda dvoinaia),*[1] but finding it hard to complete a work much longer than his accustomed short stories, he soon abandoned it altogether. The basis of
this unfinished work was to emerge eventually in his novel *The Shining
World (Blistaiushchii mir)* (1923), where the hero, Drood, bears the additional name of "Double Star" *("Dvoinaia zvezda").* It was Kipling's
story *Rikki-Tikki-Tavi* that suggested to Nina Grin the name Tavi for the
heroine—"an easy, elegant and simple name,"[2] as Grin remarked. The
writing of this novel seems to have occupied most of 1921, as only two
new tales appeared that year: *Grif*[3] and *The Competition in Liss (So-
stiazanie v Lisse).*[4] The latter, the story of an air race, was inspired by
the Aviation Week in Petersburg from 25 April to 2 May 1910, but it is
not known whether it was ever printed at that time.

Grin began *The Shining World* in the autumn of 1921. Before reading
the first two chapters to an audience in the House of Writers, he took
them to Gornfel'd, who was greatly impressed. Grin should realise, he
said, that the excellence of these chapters obliged him "to steer his creative course henceforth according to them, and not to squander his tal-
ents on trifles."[5] Repeating the critic's words to his wife, Grin went on:
'. . . things will be difficult both for you and for me, because I shall not
succeed in being published as might be hoped: the epoch demands otherwise. And as to when the direction I have taken and that of the epoch
will converge—that is unknown. But we . . . shall not be afraid and shall
travel down the road which beckons to us."[6] The accuracy of his prediction was to be proved in the late 1920s, when the Russian Association of Proletarian Writers (RAPP) controlled Soviet literature and when
Grin, though rarely able to find publishers for his work, remained true
to his artistic self.

The year 1922 saw few publications of Grin's work. Several amusing anecdotes were printed in the cheap journal *Mukhomor* ("The Death-Cap"), among them *On a Visit to a Friend (V gostiakh u priiatelia)*,[7] *Monte Cristo (Monte-Kristo)*,[8] and *A Tender Love Affair (Nezhnyi roman)*.[9] One collection of three stories entitled *White Fire (Belyi ogon')* was published, containing the tale of that name, *The Tightrope (Kanat)*,[10] and *Ships in Liss (Korabli v Lisse)*,[11] one of Grin's finest pieces.

In the summer of 1922 Grin spent several weeks in the Crimea. At the invitation of the Tiflis journal *Zaria vostoka* ("Dawn of the East"), Isaac Babel' travelled to Tiflis, and Grin appears to have accompanied him there from Odessa. The two writers apparently lived together for a while, but whereas Babel' stayed on in Tiflis as a contributor to the journal almost until the end of 1922, Grin left after no more than a month. His short story *Fourteen Feet (Chetyrnadtsat' futov)*[12] was first published in *Zaria vostoka* on 5 September 1924.[13] It is curious, however, that neither Grin nor his second wife makes any reference either to this visit to the south or to Babel'.

1923 proved a much more fruitful year than either 1921 or 1922. It brought the publication of some fifteen new works by Grin, among them *Scarlet Sails* in book form and *The Shining World* serialised in numbers 20 to 30 of the journal *Krasnaia niva* ("The Red Corn-field"). To these was added a collection of thirteen tales, comprising works such as *The Rifleman from Zurbagan (Zurbaganskii strelok)* (1913),[14] *The Seller of Happiness (Prodavets schast'ia)* (1913),[15] and *Captain Duke (Kapitan Diuk)* (1915).[16] But even in good years such as this, the couple were continually dogged by lack of money, since whatever Grin earned he invariably spent quickly and rashly. Insufficient funds forced him to decline the offer of a voyage to the Arctic Ocean in 1923, a journey he would dearly have loved to make.[17] However, the spring of 1923 brought a welcome sum in payment for recent publications, and Grin and his wife were able to take a holiday in the Crimea, visiting Sevastopol', Balaklava and Yalta, before staying in Moscow for a few days on their way home.

Their visit to the Crimea showed them the desirability of a permanent move from Petrograd to the south. Though economic and climatic factors certainly influenced their final decision, Grin's continued heavy drinking was the major consideration. In her long and totally unpublished account of Grin's alcoholism, *Grin and Wine (Grin i vino)*,[18] Nina Grin confesses that her husband's persistent drinking was the real reason for their move to the Crimea. Even after his second marriage, when he was no longer oppressed by loneliness as he had been since Vera Pavlovna's departure in 1913, Grin had never stopped drinking. He would still disappear for hours on end, frequently make a nuisance of himself, and be found drunk and often incapable on the street. Each time, his abject promises to reform would come to nothing. His wife felt that away from his boon companions in Petrograd he would find it easier to break the habit. Unfortunately, her hopes were to be only partly fulfilled. Though he drank much less after their move to the south, Grin never completely overcame the compulsion and often hid a bottle of liquor in his room so that he could drink there secretly at night.

On 6 May 1924, Grin and his wife left Petrograd for the Crimea, accompanied by Nina's widowed mother, Olga Alekseevna Mironova. Many manuscripts and rough drafts were unfortunately destroyed by Grin before their departure. Early on 10 May they arrived in Feodosia and took a room for a fortnight in the hotel "Astoria" until they could find more permanent accommodation. But their money ran out very quickly and they were forced to pawn many of their possessions. As Nina Grin recalls, this was only the beginning of a long and painful association with local money-lenders—"in whose gentle but greedy clutches we remained for six years . . . in Feodosia."[19] Although the Grins had to spend between 700 and 1,000 roubles a year paying off the interest on their loans, the money-lenders did at least enable Grin to work in peace, something which was the couple's chief concern. When the writer Vikentii Veresaev once remarked to Nina Grin that he would rather live on bread and water than line money-lenders' pockets, she replied that "without the assistance and the robbery of money-lenders, [the novels] *She Who Runs on the Waves, Jessy and Morgiana (Dzhessi i Morgiana)* [Grin's fifth novel], *The Road to Nowhere* and other works would never have been written. . . . The money-lenders were a kind of supportive wall for us, and by leaning on it Aleksandr Stepanovich could write calmly, knowing that the next day was provided for and assured, even if at the expense of privations in the future."[20] Not until they moved inland to Staryi Krym in late 1930 were the couple finally rid of the claims of their benefactors and tormentors.

In 1924 Grin began his third novel, *The Golden Chain (Zolotaia tsep')*,[21] and confessed to his wife that after the difficulties encountered in writing *The Shining World*, this much less complex work was something of a recreation: "This will be a relaxation for me; the principles of treatment on the broad canvas of a large work have become comprehensible and familiar to me. The plot, too, is simple—the memories of his dreams in a young boy who searches for miracles and finds them."[22] Within a few months the novel was completed, and Grin confided to his wife with astonishment that though he believed he had written it "without any effort at all," now that it was finished he felt utterly exhausted. "Never has such a feeling come over me upon completing a tale," he went on, "for usually when I finish writing a story, it's as if threads—albeit only of gossamer—stretch out towards a new tale, a new theme."[23] The novel was not published until the following year, 1925, when it was serialised in numbers 8 to 11 of *Novyi mir* ("New World"). Before it appeared in book form in 1926, however, Grin made substantial revisions in the work.

Perhaps his feeling of complete emptiness explains why Grin found the writing of his next novel, *She Who Runs on the Waves*,[24] so very difficult. He made over forty attempts at the beginning of the work alone, saying "I cannot easily find my way into the right channel."[25] Of these variants, only six have survived, as he burnt the remainder when he was finally satisfied with the first chapter. In all, the novel took him over eighteen months to write, from January or February 1925, until the autumn of 1926. At the end of it all he again felt utterly drained: "I am exhausted. In my mind and soul there is complete silence. However much I exert myself, not even the plot of a trivial tale occurs to me. It's just as if I were not a writer at all! While I was writing it [the novel], I felt like a rich man, so multi-coloured and brimful did my heart feel. But now, well—there's not the slightest thing."[26] For a while he even feared that with this novel his "creative ability had run dry,"[27] and that it marked the end of his literary career. Unfortunately, his difficulties were not over with the work's completion, for he now found it impossible to arrange its publication. He declared that it was a hundred times easier for him to write a novel than to "drag it through the Dantesque inferno of the publishing houses."[28] One journal returned his manuscript with the comment "highly uncontemporary and will not interest the reader,"[29] a view that prevailed until 1928, when the novel was eventually published in book form by *Zemlia i fabrika* ("Land and Factory").

Grin's next novel, *Jessy and Morgiana*,[30] was begun after a ten-month interval during which he wrote several tales, among them *Augustus Esborn's Marriage (Brak Avgusta Esborna)*,[31] *The Snake (Zmeia)*,[32] and *A Personal Technique (Lichnyi priëm)* (1926).[33] In addition, in the early summer of 1927 Grin and his wife used some of the royalties they had received to take a short holiday in the spa town of Kislovodsk in the

Caucasus.[34] When the theme of *Jessy and Morgiana* finally came to him, "like a small, weak stream that began to run from his silent soul,"[35] Grin felt immense relief. The work was finished on 20 April 1928,[36] and though the first chapters of it were rejected by *Novyi mir*, the novel was eventually published in 1929 by the *Priboi* ("Surf") publishing house in Leningrad. *Jessy and Morgiana* was to prove the least successful of his major pieces.

Despite all the difficulties of writing and publication, the couple were happy in these few brief years. However, Nina Grin found that two things were sources of constant but private pain to her: the "perpetually burning fire of alcoholism" in her husband, and his profound feeling of dissatisfaction, that of a talented man "who did not meet with real appreciation."[37] But much worse was to follow. Very soon, lawsuit and poverty, famine and fatal illness were to cloud their lives.

In February 1927, the publisher Vol'fson of the *Mysl'* ("Thought") publishing house in Leningrad had visited Grin in Feodosia and concluded with him a contract to print a full collection of his works in fifteen volumes.[38] This was to be an edition of 10,000 copies per volume, scheduled to be completed over three years. The contract would have brought Grin about 15,000 roubles. But of the projected fifteen volumes only eight actually appeared. numbers 2 and 5 in 1927, 6 and 11 in 1928, and 8, 12, 13 and 14 in 1929. The remaining seven were never published.[39] Though Grin had received some money for what had been published, he decided after much legal wrangling to sue Vol'fson for failing to fulfil his part of the contract. By law the publishing house was obliged to pay the author the full royalties agreed in the contract, if all the volumes did not appear within the stipulated time. But until the agreed three years elapsed in 1930, nothing could be done. In the meantime Grin and his wife lived from hand to mouth, borrowing money and selling what few possessions they had left. Without the money-lenders, the couple might never have survived this period.

Legal proceedings were begun in June 1929, but a year later the case had still not been settled. Nina Grin then wrote to Vera Pavlovna in Leningrad, asking her to find them a new lawyer, as they suspected their current legal adviser, a certain N. V. Krutikov,[40] of having reached a secret agreement with their influential opponent, Vol'fson.[41] Their suspicions were soon confirmed. In a letter to Vera Pavlovna on 8 July 1930, Nina Grin wrote of Krutikov: "... he's been responsible for many beastly and vile things ... he's a kind of Uriah Heep."[42]

On 13 August 1930, the case was heard in the Supreme Court in Moscow and then referred to Leningrad. There, in the late autumn of that year, Grin was finally awarded over 5,000 roubles in damages. This enabled him to settle all the debts that had accumulated in Moscow, Leningrad and Feodosia during the long legal proceedings. But when everything was paid, there was almost nothing left. Grin and his wife then decided to move from Feodosia to the little town of Staryi Krym, about twenty-five kilometres inland, where both accommodation and the cost of living were significantly cheaper. On 23 November 1930, they took a flat at 98 Lenin Street for the modest sum of 25 roubles per month.

After finishing *Jessy and Morgiana* in April 1928, Grin had rested for a fortnight before continuing work on the drafts of his last complete novel, *The Road to Nowhere*. As is the case with all his work, however, it would be quite wrong to think of separate tales and novels as having been written in strict isolation one from the next. Often he would be working on two or more pieces at the same time. This was especially the case with *Jessy and Morgiana* and *The Road to Nowhere*, and several rough drafts of both novels are to be found close together in the same manuscript.[43] Moreover, Vera Pavlovna recalls that in the winter of 1927-8 Grin wrote to her saying he was writing two novels at the same time—*The Road to Nowhere*[44] and *The Breezy Hill (Obvevaemyi kholm)* [an earlier title of *Jessy and Morgiana*]—and adding: ". . . if I grow tired of one, then I take up the other."[45] The original title of *The Road to Nowhere* was *On the Shady Side (Na tenevoi storone)*, and the work did not receive its final title until the summer of 1928, after Grin had seen the engraving "The Road to Nowhere" by the English artist John Greenwood,[46] in an exhibition in Moscow. The novel was completed in Feodosia on 23 March 1929, and issued in 1930 by the Moscow publishing house *Federatsiia* ("Federation").

The last years of Grin's life brought the dictatorship of the Russian Association of Proletarian Writers to the Soviet literary scene. Like many authors of fiction who refused to produce the writing of "social command" *(sotsial'nyi zakaz)* required by Averbakh and Bezymenskii, the militant leaders of RAPP, Grin found it almost impossible to have his work published. As early as 1926, before the worst years of RAPP's domination, he had had a foreboding of what was to come, foreseeing increasing difficulty in placing his work. "Our field is narrowing, and with every month there are fewer possibilities of my being published," he told Nina Grin at the time. "Now it's difficult to get even a story printed, never mind a novel. Soon you and I will be left alone at the centre of a narrow circle."[47] Reflecting that the epoch was whirling along and passing them by, he recalled the prophetic words spoken by Gornfel'd in the early 1920s and stubbornly refused to compromise his artistic integrity. "I can not and do not wish to be different from what I am," he maintained. "I take pleasure in the opportunity of being the writer I am. I feel distressed yet proud."[48] Asking himself the question: "When will the direction I have taken in my work coincide with that of the epoch?", he replied with unwitting accuracy: "Probably when I am gone."[49]

The three years of RAPP's domination, from 1929 to 1932, were to prove Gornfel'd's prediction correct. 1930 and 1931 were extremely difficult. In the first Grin had fewer than ten items published, among them the tales *The Story of a Hawk (Istoriia odnogo iastreba)*,[50] *The Green Lamp (Zelënaia lampa)*[51] and *Silence (Molchanie)*,[52] the novel *The Road to Nowhere*, and one collection of stories entitled *Fire and Water (Ogon' i voda)*, published by *Federatsiia*. 1931 was very much worse, however, for it saw only five publications: five of the six chapters of Grin's unfinished autobiographical record—"Escape to America" ("Begstvo v Ameriku"), "Hunter and Sailor" ("Okhotnik i matros"), "Odessa," "Baku," and "Sevastopol'"—in the journal *Zvezda*,[53] and that due only to the kindness of Tikhonov, Vol'pe and others on the editorial board. But Grin was unable to place his three new tales, *The Bet (Pari)*,[54] *The Velvet Curtain (Barkhatnaia port'era)*[55] and *The Port Commandant (Komendant porta)*,[56] and they were published only posthumously, in 1933,[57] when the dictatorship of RAPP was over.

While the RAPP organisation controlled literature, Grin was allowed to publish only one novel a year and forbidden any re-editions of work published previously. "It's just as if I were a shoemaker," he said bitterly of this ruling, "no more than one pair of shoes."[58] There can be no doubt that such restrictions affected his work and stifled his creativity. Nina Grin writes that her husband "felt suffocated, for he had insufficient spiritual scope, something without which he . . . could not write and look upon the joys of the world he loved so much."[59] Grin certainly felt profound personal distress, for he declared: "I cannot write for nobody. I must know that I have a reader—some person who is unknown and invisible to me, and yet to whom I recount my story. . . . They tell me: 'You are not in accord with the epoch, and the epoch is taking vengeance on you through us.' On what, then, do you wish me to live? After all, this is my profession, my daily bread. The incentive to carry on, the awareness that one has a reader, are fading away. I am not one of those writers who expatiate in their manuscripts: I write only about the human soul!"[60] He regarded the discrepancy between his kind of writing and that demanded by the epoch as primarily a question of artistic taste, and saw that the literary preferences of his critics were profoundly alien to his own. "They consider me less complex than I am," he said, "they love the resounding crash of contemporary life—the present day; the peaceful backwater of human feelings and souls does not interest or excite them."[61] Apropos of the pressure currently put upon authors to write not in the way they themselves wished but as others decreed, he wrote tartly to Gorky in August 1930, that if "the alto could sing the tenor part, the bass the alto, and the treble the falsetto, then the Trade Section of the State Publishing House *(Torgsektor GIZa)* would always have the appropriate unison. All this," he added darkly, "is something more than trade."[62] By the time RAPP was disbanded by Party decree on 23 April 1932, Grin was already seriously ill, and never lived to profit from the wind of literary change.

Material need alone forced Grin to embark on his last long work, *The Autobiographical Tale*, which he never finished. He did not find the writing of it particularly difficult, and each chapter was soon completed, but his profound aversion for disclosing details of his biography made it a painful exercise. Its writing, he said, was "tantamount to taking off one's last shirt and selling it."[63] Of the time when the *Tale* was written and of the process of its writing, Nina Grin recalls: "It was with mental suffering and loathing that Aleksandr Stepanovich wrote his autobiographical stories. Necessity forced him to do it . . . those were the most wretched years, 1930 and 1931. . . . this book of mental suffering about the misfortunes of his difficult youth—relived in the writing of it—was never completed, for he had insufficient strength to do it."[64] The only thing in his autobiography which Grin anticipated pleasure in describing was his "Bohemian time" with Kuprin, but the *Tale* unfortunately never reached that period of his life.

He began work on his autobiography at the beginning of 1930, first giving it the title *By Land and Sea (Na sushe i more)*, with the sub-title *Autobiographical Sketches by A. S. Grin (Avtobiograficheskie ocherki A. S. Grina)*. There is evidence to suggest that he also wished to call it *A Book about Myself (Kniga o sebe)*.[65] *Legend about Myself (Legenda o sebe)* was the title of a foreword he intended to put to the work, and he sent the manuscript of this to the critic Tsezar Vol'pe. As this foreword indicates, Grin was only too well aware of the legends that had grown up around his name: "Between 1906 and 1930 I heard from fel-

9. Two letters from Grin to Vladimir Lidin, one dated 7 October 1924, the other dated 31 October with no year given. It seems reasonable to assume that the second letter also belongs to 1924. (Gifts from the private collection of Vladimir Lidin.)

10. "The rough road that comes up from Grassington and goes to no-
    where." The engraving by the Yorkshireman, John Greenwood,
    which inspired the title of Grin's last novel, *The Road to Nowhere
    (Doroga nikuda)* (1930). (Greenwood, J. F., *The Dales Are Mine*,
    London, 1952, facing p. 96.)

low-writers so many amazing reports about myself that I began to have doubts as to whether I had really lived in the way I have described here. . . . I shall recount what I heard as though I were speaking for myself. Voyaging as a sailor somewhere near Zurbagan, Liss and San-Riol' [three of Grin's imagined ports in his *Grinlandia*], Grin killed an English captain and seized a chest of manuscripts written by him. . . . Grin pretends that he knows no foreign languages, but in fact he knows them well. . . . He did not restrict himself to one victim. After killing the captain, he murdered his first wife and then escaped from penal servitude in exile, to which he had been sentenced for twelve years."[66] Since he believed that readers would regard even his truthful autobiography as an invention, Grin finally decided to call the entire work *Legend about Myself*. When the *Izdatel'stvo pisatelei v Leningrade* ("The Writers' Publishing House in Leningrad") and not he himself gave the work its comparatively uninspired present title, Grin—by then already ill—said with a bitter smile: "They're either afraid to stick their necks out or they think the reader will doubt whether this is a real autobiography. Miserable creatures . . . they won't believe anything, not even that I'm ill."[67]

It seems that his last completed novel, *The Road to Nowhere*, gave Grin the idea for his next novel, *Touch-Me-Not (Nedotroga)*, which was left unfinished at his death. On completing the former he told his wife that from it "the theme of 'touch-me-nots' was born." "The subject of it is important and one that moves me profoundly," he went on. "There are many such touch-me-nots, but they hide themselves away and are inconspicuous; yet they are often very beautiful, like miracle-flowers."[68] Although his thoughts on the new work were clear, however, the plot formed only with great difficulty in his mind. "I think it over," he said, "and I see everything vividly, . . . but when I begin to write there is no inner harmony."[69]

He began *Touch-Me-Not* no later than December 1930. In a letter to Vera Pavlovna on the 6th, Nina Grin said that he was writing his autobiography, "and in fits and starts *Touch-Me-Not*."[70] On 23 December, when the six chapters of the *Autobiographical Tale* were almost finished, she wrote: "He very much wants to set to work soon on the novel *Touch-Me-Not* . . . for a year and a half now, out of [financial] necessity, he hasn't written a novel, but in his soul he's longing to do so."[71] Judging from extant rough drafts of this unfinished work[72] (chiefly its first two chapters), where the plot and characters are already defined, there is no reason to suppose that at the end of his life Grin was in any way departing from his accustomed romantic technique of which RAPP so disapproved.

He had first thought of *Touch-Me-Not* early in 1930, and for almost two years he wrestled with it, assuring his wife that it would be "better and more powerful than *She Who Runs on the Waves*."[73] The demands of RAPP that he write only of "the contemporary and the everyday"[74] were largely responsible for his difficulties in writing the work, for he feared it might never be published even if it were completed. No doubt, too, his deteriorating health increased his sense of disillusionment. However, in the last months of his life he was briefly to regain some of his former vigour, and rapidly wrote the children's South American adventure story, *The "Stone Pillar" Ranch (Rancho "Kamennyi stolb")*.[75]

Having won their lawsuit with the *Mysl'* publishing house in 1930, Grin and his wife reckoned that the money left after their debts were paid would last them another year. But they had not taken into account the famine then beginning in the Crimea and the consequent sharp rise in the price of food. As a result, by August 1931 they were almost starving. An attempt made by Grin to take a job as a geography teacher failed: he was rejected on political grounds because of his previous association with the SR Party. So desperate were the couple for money that Grin then decided to travel alone to Moscow—his wife could not afford to accompany him—in order to claim in person the royalties due for the chapters of his *Autobiographical Tale* published in *Zvezda* earlier that year.

Successful in obtaining the 600 roubles owed to him, he returned to Staryi Krym on 21 August 1931, in a state of severe exhaustion. While in the north he had visited Leningrad and had indulged in what was probably the worst drinking bout of his life. After being found lying insensible behind a fence, he had been taken into the House of Scholars to recover. Nina Grin's account *Grin and Wine* contains a vivid and detailed description of the unfortunate episode. Apart from the after-effects of this, however, Grin was certainly already ill when he returned home. At first he was thought to be suffering from a renewed attack ·of malaria. Then inflammation of the lungs was diagnosed and a further investigation suggested tuberculosis. X-rays indicated an infected right lung.

Disappointment and depression undoubtedly contributed to his poor physical condition. While in Moscow he had again failed to find a publisher for his three new tales, *The Bet*, *The Velvet Curtain* and *The Port Commandant*, and had realised that his literary affairs were generally in a bad state. Moreover, he had heard that his works were being "unofficially" removed from the shelves of Moscow libraries because the RAPP organisation considered them undesirable reading. But he still refused to accede to the current demands for literature of "social command." Never, he insisted, could he become a writer of factual industrial sketches *(ocherkist)* in the way that so many of his fellow-authors had obediently done: "I find the industrial sketch completely detestable, since my soul is not fond of any kind of engineering or mechanics on a mass scale. I can take interest in an individual specialist, a craftsman jeweller who is master of his art, . . . but I find totally uninteresting the engineer of machine-tools, electrical plants and ball-bearings, factories, works and other supreme vanities."[76] He recalled that his tale *The Opener of Locks (Otkryvatel' zamkov),* first published in 1929,[77] was a concession to this type of writing which he so disliked. Need alone had forced him to produce a work that he now considered no more than "a worthless compilation"[78] and a private lapse. Whatever his critics might think, he preferred to go on writing in his own particular way, declaring. "To write as I write—though people say it is a 'narrow' road—at least it is *my* road," and adding that to the end of his days he wished only to wander through what he called "the bright lands of my own imagination."[79]

In late August 1931, he wrote to the Union of Writers, asking whether he might be given a pension because his illness was preventing him from working: "I am now 51. My health is in ruins, my material situation is one of poverty, and my capacity for work has fallen sharply. For two years now I have been working on a new novel, *Touch-Me-Not,* but do not know how soon I shall manage to finish it. I have no royalties still to come. We have eaten up our last 50 roubles."[80] Furthermore, he wrote, that coming November was to see the twenty-fifth anniversary of his literary début. His letter to the Union brought no reply, but fortunately in October the poet Tikhonov sent a gift of 300 roubles and in November a congratulatory telegram—the only one—on Grin's literary anniversary.

Though his health was deteriorating rapidly, help was not forthcoming from any other fellow-writers, still less from the Union, and a letter to Gorky sent via the poet Georgii Shengeli brought no response. Embittered by the almost total lack of outside help, Grin felt forgotten in his hour of need. Nina Grin's regular letters to Vera Pavlovna throughout her husband's fatal illness convey a vivid and painful impression of the couple's plight. Forced to buy medicines and specially nutritious food that they could barely afford, Nina and her mother sold everything they possibly could. "We have no money," she wrote to Vera Pavlovna on 3 November 1931, "they don't know what Aleksandr's illness is and it preys on our minds; we're selling our things with difficulty for next to nothing, and we have no idea what's in store for us."[81]

The illness that Grin had at first cheerfully believed was sent him "as a salutary punishment"[82] now brought him severe rheumatic pains. He became increasingly gloomy and depressed in the house where they lived, saying that he longed for "a little bit of sunshine"[83] in his room. His condition deteriorated so rapidly that by the end of March 1932, he could no longer remain sitting in a chair and was forced to stay in bed. His wife considered moving him to the clinic of the House of Scholars in Leningrad, but was advised against it as conditions and food there apparently left much to be desired. Eventually the Union of Writers wrote that a place might be arranged in a Yalta sanatorium, but nothing more was actually done. In April 1932, Grin wrote what were to be his last lines:

> I am ill and weak—but my love is not ailing,
> And my memory of the past is not failing.[84]

When he read in a newspaper later that month of the disbanding of RAPP, he said joyfully to his wife that henceforth life would be easier for them: "There's been a breath of fresh air . . . they've broken up the Averbakh gang."[85]

Feeling that a move to more agreeable accommodation might halt her husband's rapid decline, Nina Grin succeeded after much difficulty in exchanging her gold watch (a gift from Grin and her most treasured possession) for a little house at number 52 Liebknecht Street. The house had a pleasant garden, faced south and was always full of light, and is today a museum *(dom-muzei)* devoted to Grin. When the couple moved into their new home on 6 June 1932, the change of scene and the more pleasant surroundings brought an immediate though brief improvement in Grin. He felt cheerful and his thoughts turned to work in this new setting that he liked so much. "Here I shall write my *Touch-Me-Not*," he declared, "this will be our paradise."[86] Shortly afterwards, only three weeks before his death, he was still thinking about his new novel, saying to his wife that the work had "finally crystallised" in his imagination, and that some scenes in it were so good that, as he put it, "recalling them, I smile at them."[87]

Despite his euphoria, though, Grin was wasting away before his wife's eyes. Already in early May she had written to Vera Pavlovna: "His muscles have practically disappeared, and only the bones and tendons are left."[88] The couple's material situation had improved slightly, however, as Veresaev had sent them a gift of 200 roubles in April and Vera Pavlovna gave them smaller amounts as and when she could. But Grin grew steadily more feeble, and when in June twenty-five author's copies of his *Autobiographical Tale* arrived from Leningrad, he was almost too weak to read the title page. Sensing the approach of death, he said: "I do not wish for it, but I am not afraid."[89]

Yet even after all this time his doctors were still unable to decide exactly what his illness was, suggesting variously anaemia, tuberculosis, rheumatic fever and extreme nervous exhaustion. Finally, after a consilium of two doctors and a specialist, cancer of the stomach was diagnosed on 30 June, and Grin was declared a hopeless case. Henceforth, brandy and milk were his only sustenance, and morphia his only solace in increasing pain.

On 6 July he asked for a priest and took Communion. On the morning of 8 July he lost consciousness and died at half-past six that evening. After all his suffering, Nina Grin could well say that "to his wretched lot there fell both a painful illness and a difficult death."[90] During the funeral the following evening about two hundred people followed the coffin to the church and many more lined the route, while crowds gathered in the little cemetery of Staryi Krym. But the only relatives present were Nina Grin and her mother, and no literary figures came to pay their last respects. The poet Maksimilian Voloshin, who lived not far away in Koktebel' on the coast and knew Grin well, was unable to attend, and indeed was to die himself only a few weeks later. In dire financial straits, Nina Grin buried her husband with the last of the royalties received for his *Autobiographical Tale*.

*　　　*　　　*

Like the greater part of Grin's life, this second marriage had been far from easy. Hardly a year had passed without the couple's being beset by acute financial difficulties, while the menace of drink had always been Nina Grin's private Damoclean sword. Almost three months after Grin's death she confessed to Vera Pavlovna that their marriage had been very difficult. "All the same," she added, "how much poetry there was in it! . . . its only blemish was Aleksandr's alcoholism and its effects."[91] Later she was to admit that Grin always had an idealised image of what a woman and wife should be, and that she had constantly striven to adhere as closely as possible to that image, though basically she was not at all the person he imagined. In her letter to Vera Pavlovna of 5 April 1938 she wrote: "He idealised me very much, and even at the beginning of our life together . . . I saw this clearly. . . . I promised myself that in my life with Aleksandr Stepanovich I would try to conform with his ideal image so as not to disillusion him."[92] But this was difficult, she explained: "I simply possessed two or three traits which coincided with his ideal of a woman, whereas he looked upon me as his complete ideal."[93]

Whether Grin had a preconceived notion of his ideal woman or not, the fact remains that Nina Nikolaevna was personally responsible for affording him during the eleven years of their marriage a measure of peace and contentment greater than he had ever known. Moreover, she enabled him to work far more systematically and productively than ever before. Left to his own devices in Petrograd in the early 1920s, he would probably have become a chronic alcoholic and frittered away his immense talent amid squalor and degradation, a state to which he was already dangerously close when he married Nina Nikolaevna in 1921. There can be little doubt that without her, the Grin we know today could never have been. For the man who was so often intensely lonely and withdrawn, she was a loyal and understanding friend, while for the author who was almost always underestimated and misunderstood, she proved a source of constant encouragement and inspiration.

EPILOGUE

> "Grin is talented and very
> interesting; it is a pity that
> he is so little appreciated."
> Maxim Gorky[1]

Aleksandr Grin's début in Russian literature came at a time when Chekhov, Gorky, Andreev, Bunin and Kuprin dominated the literary stage. An anomaly because of his technique, subject matter and style, Grin was largely restricted to the pages of less prestigious journals and newspapers until the early 1920s. Though his first novella, *Scarlet Sails*, was not published until 1923, when he was already forty-three, the decade that followed before his death produced many works of high quality—five short novels and some seventy tales. Mercifully, death spared him the trials of Socialist Realism shortly to be visited upon Soviet writers. There is every reason to suppose that he would have found Zhdanov's literary strait-jacket intolerably constricting.

Throughout his life Grin went unrecognised not only by the majority of critics but also by most contemporary writers. Arkadii Gornfel'd's two articles in *Russkoe bogatstvo* were rare exceptions to the general rule.[2] The great defect of almost all criticism of Grin's work during his lifetime was its failure to perceive the moral and spiritual values central to his *Weltanschauung*. The overwhelming majority of commentators saw in him little more than a skilful imitator of the adventure genre as practised in the West, and failed to see that he simply used the conventions of that genre as a bridge to an infinitely more original philosophical purpose. Critics' opinions—themselves largely the product of insufficient perception—were transmitted to readers of Grin, so helping to perpetuate a false notion of him that sadly has survived, though in a somewhat less rigid form, to the present day. In the late Stalin period Grin was attacked as a rootless cosmopolitan and bourgeois reactionary, and his works were declared undesirable reading. Only since the "Thaw" has his writing enjoyed the critical attention it deserves.

As Grin's novels and the majority of his romantic tales show, dream and fantasy constitute the *raison d'être* of his heroes.[3] What most concerns him is not so much that his heroes should fulfil their dreams by transforming fantasy into reality, as that they should safeguard their aspirations and preserve them intact. Only unremitting persistence in their ideal can reward Grinlandians with the realisation of their dreams. Moreover, their aspirations must be sufficiently robust to withstand any attempt to destroy them. Since their dreams of an exclusive destiny arise from an unsympathetic or even hostile reality, the obstacles raised against them in the real environment serve to test the strength and durability of their convictions.

The advent of their special destiny is foreshadowed in the lives of Grin's heroes by the sudden appearance of the extraordinary, taking the form of exciting adventure or intriguingly novel experience. Grin attached great importance to the sudden way in which the unexpected irrupts into the usually drab lives of his characters. As he once wrote in a rough draft: "Unexpectedness has the capacity to turn the most ordinary of occurrences into something splendid. For instance: food suddenly discovered in the Sahara."[4] Moreover, the element of surprise is heightened by the fact that the characters through whose agency the extraordinary appears are usually completely unfamiliar to Grin's heroes. However, this does not prevent the latter from accurately assessing what kind of people the strangers are. The Grinian hero's uncanny ability to define the significance of those who purvey the extraordinary derives from his rare perception and sensitivity, qualities which intensify his organic longing for the exclusive.

The accuracy of the hero's assessment is demonstrated by the exceptional events which swiftly follow the strangers' appearance. The vindication of the hero's faith in the eventual fulfilment of his dream—a vindication seen in the actual arrival of the exclusive—establishes a relationship of affection and trust between the hero and the agents of the extraordinary. Grin's hero may even become a grateful follower of those who have designed his felicity, and may share with them the spiritual delights of exceptional experience.

Grin believes that when they are engendered by a *romanesque* imagination and, wherever possible, applied to creative effect in extraordinary adventure or exclusive experience, dream and fantasy have a positive ethical value. They not only serve as a priceless source of inspiration for the happy few who enjoy them, but also act as a resilient spiritual buffer against the insensitive majority who are hostile towards them. The ethical importance that Grin attaches to the dream explains why his dreamer-hero is first and foremost an allegorical figure attesting the potential of aspiration, rather than a life-like creature of flesh and blood. Thus Grin's romantic heroes are central to an ideal philosophical system which asserts the value of spiritual integrity and steadfast aspiration. Of prime importance in that system and forming the basis of Grin's *Weltanschauung* is his belief that man has a duty to dream of a romantic ideal, and that he should treat his dream not flippantly but as seriously as he regards the visible reality around him. Only unflinching faith in the realisation of one's dream can make it come true, Grin believes, by transforming the extraordinary and apparently impossible into something ordinary and essentially possible. This contrast between the impossible and the possible—one that underlies much of Grin's romantic work—is stated in simple terms by Grey of *Scarlet Sails*, when he refers to the way in which he is fulfilling the heroine's dream: "I'm doing what exists as an age-old notion of the beautiful and impossible, but which is, in essence, just as feasible and possible as a walk in the country."[5] So it is that miracles in Grin come about not in the transcendental sphere of abstract fantasy, but in the thoroughly workaday circumstances of terrestrial reality. Consequently, once the miracle has become manifest, neither its fictional beneficiary nor Grin's reader finds it very hard to believe in an occurrence that seems so eminently possible.

In his study of Soviet science fiction, Anatolii Britikov devotes several pages to Grin.[6] Though Grin was not familiar with science as many of his literary contemporaries—notably Aleksei Tolstoi—were, Britikov believes that he has a definite place in the history of Russian science fiction. The miraculous element in Grin's work, he writes, is inspired with faith in man—man in the highest sense of the word—and that faith is closely related to the spirit of true science fiction. But it is important to note that unlike most science fiction writers, Grin is never concerned as to how precisely his miracles come about. He gives no "scientific" explanations and never resorts to mysticism in an attempt to obscure the event. What concerns him most is the moral or spiritual metaphor contained in the miraculous happening, and so the actual way in which the event comes about is essentially irrelevant to his artistic purpose. Thus it is the symbolic value of Grin's miracles that is paramount. When Iurii Olesha congratulated him on the excellent suitability of the flying man theme (in Grin's work *The Shining World*) for use in a novel of fantasy, Grin retorted: "What do you mean, for a fantastic novel? It's a symbolic novel, not a fantastic one! It's not a man flying at all—it's the soaring of the spirit!"[7]

Though traditional science fiction writers like Jules Verne and H. G. Wells produced "socio-technological" fantasy, while Grin wrote what might be termed "socio-ethical" fantasy (which includes no purely scientific material), all three authors believed in the impossible because they had faith in the boundless creative potential of man. All three took their readers' imaginations deep into the wonders of nature and the miracles of the human spirit, and in so doing defied the notorious "common sense" that too often shackles man's limitless capacity for discovery and innovation. Grin exercised an important though largely indirect influence on Russian literature of the fantastic, Britikov maintains, since his work helped to reinforce the human as against the scientific element in Russian fantasy writing. He should therefore be seen as a vital link between the great Russian realistic tradition whose prime concern is the study of man, and the machine and science-oriented fantasy literature of the mid-twentieth century.

The popular notion of Grin as a pure romantic wholly divorced from the reality of his native Russia is to some degree belied by his realistic tales which derive from his SR experiences in the early 1900s. Though his *Grinlandia* was to a great extent an imaginative reaction against the philistinism of Viatka, it was never a means of deliberate spiritual emigration from his homeland. This was the false charge levelled at Grin by the critics Vazhdaev[8] and Tarasenkov[9] in their violent attacks upon him in 1950, when such lasting damage was done to his literary reputation. A brief examination of their remarks will help to show the kind of unfair criticism to which Grin's work was subjected during the late Stalin period. Denouncing what he called the "cult" of Grin among Soviet intellectuals, Vazhdaev damned the writer as a bourgeois cosmopolitan who felt no love for his native Russia. The devised setting of his works, the critic wrote, was nothing more than an ideal cosmopolitan paradise, a cunning literary camouflage behind which bourgeois tradition and social inequality could live on undisturbed. Vazhdaev accused Grin of not wishing to reflect Soviet actuality in his writing because he was hostile to the regime, and even went so far as to classify him with the White *émigré* poet, Vladislav Khodasevich, whose hostility to the USSR was beyond dispute. For his part, Tarasenkov condemned Grin as an archreactionary and anti-nationalist writer who had turned his back squarely on the great realistic tradition of Russian literature. How, he asked, did Grin's priorities differ from the literary credo of the Serapion Brethren in the early 1920s, with its insistence that a work of art is not necessarily any the worse if it does not reflect its epoch? Tarasenkov concluded that

Grin's literary technique was essentially a subtly disguised and therefore potentially more dangerous restatement of the Serapions' manifesto.

In view of such criticisms, it is important to remember that *Grinlandia* began to develop as a setting for Grin's romantic fiction long before 1917. Tales such as *Reno Island* and *The Lanfier Colony*, published in 1909 and 1910 respectively, show beyond all doubt that Vazhdaev is mistaken in thinking *Grinlandia* was an escapist device invented only after the Bolshevik Revolution. Moreover, *Grinlandia* is not a Utopia as the critic asserts, though it is true that its geographical "isolation" and imaginary character owe something to the traditional ideal commonwealth.[10] *Grinlandia's* society is not at all exemplary and her people are far from perfect; like the real world beyond her shores, she has her men of venality and evil. Nor is *Grinlandia* a specifically *capitalist* Utopia as Vazhdaev maintains. Grin not only makes no attempt to conceal defects of the capitalist system in his imaginary setting, but also frequently exaggerates them so as to provide motives for his heroes' actions in defence of morality and justice. His last novel, *The Road to Nowhere*, illustrates this best, for its hero is forced to contend with the concerted opposition of a bribed judiciary and corrupt bureaucracy. In interpreting Grin's work in crudely sociological and political terms, both Vazhdaev and Tarasenkov failed to perceive one of its most fundamental preoccupations: transcending all boundaries, be they political or social, it aims at the humanitarian service of all men.

Not until 1956 was the critical balance somewhat redressed, with the publication of Mark Shcheglov's short article on Grin in *Novyi mir.*[11] The critic affirmed that Grin's work demonstrated not a rejection of real life but a more creative and vital attitude towards it. "Grin's romance," he wrote, "should be seen not as a withdrawal from life [*ukhod ot zhizni*] but as an entry [*prikhod*] into it, with all the fascination and excitement of faith in the goodness and beauty of man. . . ."[12]

The secret of the extraordinary popularity which Grin's work has always enjoyed in Soviet Russia—most of all during the late Stalin period when his works were in virtually clandestine circulation in Moscow and Leningrad—perhaps lies, as Zavalishin suggests, in the strong assertion of their individuality by his heroes.[13] Elizabeth Beaujour argues that Grin's attraction stems from the fact that his writing is permeated by a belief in unsuspected and extraordinary potential, a belief "incarnate in the pure of heart."[14] The moral purity of Grin's work—what she terms his "morality of total individual honesty and sincerity"[15]—makes it very relevant to present Soviet conditions, in which Russians are still wrestling with the legacy of hypocrisy and deceit left by the Stalinist age.

It seems to me, however, that the continuing fascination which Grin holds for Soviet readers does not derive primarily from their desire to offset the effects of recent social traumas. Through his work Grin gives them the opportunity to experience life with an intensity and immediacy that the constrained nature of modern existence rarely allows. Thus *Grinlandia* is much more than a gorgeously exotic setting where strenuous adventure and romantic love await those who escape from the real world. It is an environment geographically and politically independent of actuality, where fundamental human qualities may be openly demonstrated and where the forces of good may fearlessly engage those of evil. Since they are not political but moral and spiritual, the problems Grin poses and the solutions he offers are of universal significance, pertaining to the human condition. Grin believes that by spiritual strength and conviction man can turn his romantic ideal into living fact. In acquiring the dimensions and authenticity of an additional sub-continent, his *Grinlandia* became the environment where romantic visions could miraculously be transformed into reality.

Perhaps the best service that any student of Aleksandr Grin can render him is incontrovertibly to refute the widely-held and damaging notion that in his writing he deserted his native Russia. In her biography of her husband, Nina Grin recalls the destructive articles written by Vazhdaev and Tarasenkov, and asks whether Grin really did forsake Russia in his work. Her reply is an eloquent and convincing denial: "No, he did not leave Russia. And he never did. He lived in his native country, knew and loved it, and, most important of all, saw it in a way others rarely see it. . . . His settings are Russian settings—of Viatka and the Urals, Archangel, the Caucasus and the Crimea, especially Sevastopol' and Yalta; and [his characters] are Slavs—with their steadfast firmness, their tenacity in the pursuit of their goal, . . . their gentleness, trustfulness, kindness of heart, and their tremendous ability to endure hardship and suffering."[16] Thus Grin does not decline to portray Russian reality in his work, but portrays it in a way which is extremely uncharacteristic of Russian literature. Hence the general assumption, particularly early in his career, that he was little more than a gifted imitator of Western models. It is precisely his highly peculiar view of people and things—as Nina Grin puts it: *"on . . . videl tak, kak redko kto vidit"*[17]—which gives rise to the strongly "translated" quality of his writing. What both critics and readers have usually failed to see is that the atypical nature of his work does not *prove* that he declined to draw upon his native environment for his fiction.

Throughout his career Grin was very much aware of the foreign fla-
vour associated with his writing. Yet he was never in any doubt that his
technique had its roots deep in the Russian life around him. In her memoirs Nina Grin has recorded what he said one day in 1926 when he no-
ticed a beautiful vine branch growing over picturesque, stony ruins near
Otuzy, not far from Staryi Krym. Her few lines contain the very essence
of Grin's literary technique. Gazing at the vine, he said:

"Here now, I'll describe it as I see it, then people will read what I
have written and it will seem to them that this is in some unfamiliar foreign land. But it's here, nearby, close to my very eyes and
soul. And everything is like that. What matters is how you look at
it. My eyes and senses perceive it in a way which someone else
does not notice, and that is why it seems not to belong here. And
my characters, too, devoid of obligatory *couleur locale* [sic], seem
not to belong here either, but they are around us all the time. I
see them, feel and describe in entirety their emotions, desires and
experiences, unclouded by details of everyday life, politics or other
accretions. They live, suffer, are happy, and move the reader."[18]

The visionary's own words are perhaps the best retort to his detractors
and the most telling vindication of his literary technique.

APPENDIX A

Four letters from A. S. Grin to A. M. Gor'kii. First published in Russian, without reference to archive location, in Vl. Sandler, ed., *Vospominaniia ob Aleksandre Grine* (Leningrad: "Lenizdat," 1972). Given here as found in the IMLI holdings in 1970 and translated by the author of the present biography.

1. Date unknown, but probably Spring, 1909.
Source: IMLI, *Arkhiv Gor'kogo*, KG-P, 22, 3, 1, list 1.

Deeply honoured Aleksei Maksimovich!

I write to you of my own volition and on the advice of V. A. Posse.*
I am a writer of fiction, have had works published for more than two years now, and want very much to produce a small book of my tales, which now amount to 20 or 25. Of these, 8 were printed in *Russkaia mysl'* ("Russian Thought"), *Novyi zhurnal dlia vsekh* ("The New Journal for All"), *Obrazovanie* ("Education"), *Novoe slovo* ("The New Word") and *Bodroe slovo* ("The Cheerful Word"). The rest appeared in newspapers.

But as I am known to no one, as it is now spring, and as I need money, editors either refuse me or offer conditions that are unfavourable to the point of humiliation. For a long time now I have wanted to apply to you with a most humble request to examine my material and, if it is worthy of publication, to publish it in *Znanie* ("Knowledge"). As I am more uncertain than hopeful, I have not turned to you until today, but now I have made up my mind to do so. This is why I have done it: V. A. Posse has persistently recommended me to write to you, saying that most probably you subscribe to *Novyi zhurnal dlia vsekh* and have read my tales in it: *Paradise, Reno Island* and *The Story of a Conspiracy*.

---

*Vladimir Aleksandrovich Posse, a well-known journalist, close friend of Gor'-kii, and general editor of the Marxist magazine *Zhizn'* ("Life"). He was a shareholder in the *Znanie* ("Knowledge") co-operative publishing concern based in St. Petersburg and assisted Gor'kii in the editing of publications.

"And so," he said, "judging by these pieces Aleksei Maksimovich will decide whether it's worth publishing you and will give you a quick answer."

Perhaps Posse is wrong and perhaps you have not read them, but I beg you most urgently to write and say whether I should send you all my stories or whether those above are enough. The reason I am not sending them all to you now is that I have only one copy of each of them. Moreover, since I do not know what decision you may arrive at, I shall be unable to arrange their publication here in the meantime; besides, a parcel takes longer than a letter. In any case, I beg you to reply to me, by telegram if possible, so that I can if necessary send you the material quickly and receive a definite answer from you. I hope you will not be angry with me for suggesting a telegram. You understand *why* I have to ask for one.

Yours, A. S. Grin.

Aleksei Alekseevich Mal'ginov.
No. 3, Sofiiskaia Street,
Shuvalovo, St. Petersburg.

2. Dated 26 April 1920.
Source: IMLI, *Arkhiv Gor'kogo*, KG-P, 22, 3, 3, listy 1-2.

Dear Aleksei Maksimovich!

I have begun to show symptoms of typhus and am leaving today for some hospital. I beg you—if you wish to save me, then arrange an advance to me of 3,000 roubles, with which you can buy some honey and send it to me quickly. The fact is that with a high temperature (mine is 38 to 40 degrees), honey is the only way—as I have previously discovered —of causing the heavy perspiration which is so beneficial. Once, in Moscow (in 1918), being dreadfully ill with Spanish -'flu, I spent the whole night sitting over the samovar with honey, ate about 1½ pounds of it and got thoroughly soaked in sweat, but by morning I was well again.

At the Smol'nyi Infirmary you will find out where they have sent me.

In a second letter is my will. My wife lives at Flat 25, No. 17b, Zverinskaia Street, but she has not yet returned from Kazan' and I've not heard from her for a long time.

With profound gratitude,
A. Grin.

Testament
Being of sound mind and clear memory, in the event of my death I bequeath all rights of ownership of all my literary works, wherever such might be published, and likewise those as yet unpublished, exclusively and wholly to my wife, Vera Pavlovna Grinevskaia.

Aleksandr Stepanovich Grinevskii–"A. S. Grin."
26 April 1920.
Smol'nyi Infirmary, St. Petersburg

3. Dated 29 July 1920.
Source: IMLI, *Arkhiv Gor'kogo*, KG-P, 22, 3, 4, list 1.

Deeply respected Aleksei Maksimovich!
The bearer of this letter, Vera Pavlovna Grinevskaia, would like to write one of the biographies planned by the Z. I. Grzhebin publishing house (Copernicus, Galvani, Volta and others still to be decided). However, being embarrassed by the fact that this section is now out of the hands of S. F. Ol'denburg* and under the control of Mr. Pinkevich,† who will not arrive until the end of August, she has made up her mind to turn to you for instructions, advice and clarification as to whether such work is possible for her.

Knowing in literature no partiality for anyone whatsoever, by virtue of that fact I consider myself entitled to write this letter to you, a letter I would write for any author if I knew that he wished and was able to carry out work conscientiously, with flair and interest, I would write it because I consider the desire to work in accordance with one's abilities a highly laudable desire that arises from a pure source.

V. P. Grinevskaia has written for *Vskhody* ("Corn-Shoots"), *Detskii otdykh* ("Children's Rest"), *Vseobshchii zhurnal* ("The Universal Journal"), *Chital'nia narodnoi shkoly* ("The Reading-Room of the People's School"), *Tropinka* ("The Path"), *Protalinka* ("The Little Thawed Patch"), *Nedelia "Sovremennogo Slova"* ("The Week of the 'Contemporary Word'"), and *Chto i kak chitat' detiam* ("What and How to Read to Children").

---

*Sergei Fëdorovich Ol'denburg, a prominent Oriental scholar and Academician who was involved in several of Gor'kii's undertakings.

†Albert Petrovich Pinkevich, a professor, writer and expert pedagogue who worked for the Central Commission for the Improvement of Living Conditions of Scholars.

When people write a letter such as this, it is clear that its bearer is timid, is terrified of complex relations with editorial offices, and looks askance and with distrust at his own work.

I have taken into consideration everything that you have written on my manuscript, and I disagree only with your reproaching me for Averchenkoism,[§] since he laughs *downwards*, whilst I laugh *upwards*. However, do not take this as an excess of pride in me, but merely as an inclination of the neck.

I must confess to you as well that I love to find your comments on my manuscript, for in them I see and value your attention of which I am completely undeserving.

As regards the scene in which Smith is hired,[‡] I must say that it is vitally necessary for what follows, but I will correct all the beginning of it and will partly rewrite it.

Whereupon, with a request to forgive me for the hindrance I have caused you in your general work, I remain, *as always*, yours truly,

A. S. Grin.

29 July 1920. St. Petersburg.

4. Dated 7 May 1921.
Source: IMLI, *Arkhiv Gor'kogo*, KG-P, 22, 3, 6, listy 2-3.

Deeply respected Aleksei Maksimovich!

Forgive me for troubling you. I write to you with a most humble request. Be so good as to look through the contents of the two enclosed pieces of paper, and if you do not find them strange for any reason, then please ratify the text of them with your signature, and with the addition of just a few of those lines of yours which already more than once have alleviated my wretched life.

I have gained the impression that you have no free moments even at home, and that is why, not venturing to disturb you personally, I am sending this letter.

With my complete and devoted esteem,

A. Grin.

7 May 1921.

[§] Arkadii Timofeevich Averchenko, journalist, playwright and author, editor of the humorous weekly periodical *Novyi satirikon* ("The New Satyricon") from 1913 to 1918.

[‡] Part of Grin's unfinished novel *The Mysterious Circle (Tainstvennyi krug)*.

Be so good, Aleksei Maksimovich, to send your reply, if there should be one, to the Grzhebin publishing house.

P.S. A *third* request—one that will surprise you very much—is this. In about six or seven days, I am to enter into lawful matrimony. Will you not make me happy by helping me to procure somewhere just one bottle of *spirits*?

APPENDIX B

One hitherto unpublished letter from A. M. Gor'kii and E. Zamiatin to A. S. Grin.

Dated 8 March 1921.
Source: IMLI, *Arkhiv Gor'kogo*, B10, 21, 3, 10, list 1.

Р.С.Ф.С.Р.
„Дом Искусств"
при
Комисс. Народного Просв.
Комитет отдел.

8 марта 1921 г.
Петроград, Мойка, 59.   А. С. Грину

Комитет ДОМА ИСКУССТВ ставит Вас в известность, что комитетом неоднократно получались заявления о Вашем грубом обращении с служащими и площадных ругательствах по их адресу. Комитет выражает Вам по этому поводу свое негодование и заявляет, что он не может никому из жильцов ДОМА ИСКУССТВ позволить такого обращения с служащими. В виду этого Комитет предлагает Вам в месячный срок подыскать себе помещение вне стен ДОМА ИСКУССТВ.

ПРЕДСЕДАТЕЛЬ КОМИТЕТА (подпись) М. Горький.
СЕКРЕТАРЬ (подпись) Е. Замятин.
С подлинным верно: Я. Иоффе.

R.S.F.S.R.
"House of Arts",
under the
Commission for Popular Education,
Committee Section.

8 March 1921.
59, Moika, Petrograd.

To: A. S. Grin.

The Committee of the House of Arts informs you that it has repeatedly received complaints about your rude treatment of employees [of the institution] and the foul oaths which you have used to them. In this connection the Committee expresses its indignation and declares that it cannot permit any members of the House of Arts to treat employees in this way. In view of this, the Committee requires you within one month's time to find yourself accommodation outside the House of Arts.

Chairman of the Committee (signed) M. Gor'kii.
Secretary (signed) E. Zamiatin.
Certified true copy: Ia. Ioffe.

LIST OF ABBREVIATIONS USED IN THE NOTES

BS   Aleksandr Grin, *Belyi shar* (Rasskazy i povesti) (Moscow: "Molodaia gvardiia," 1966).

DM   A. S. Grin, *Dzhessi i Morgiana* (Povest', novelly, roman) (Leningrad: "Lenizdat," 1966).

FD   Aleksandr Grin, *Fandango* (Roman, povesti i rasskazy, avtobiograficheskie ocherki) (Simferopol': Izd-vo "Krym," 1966).

NNG   Nina Nikolaevna Grin, "Zapiski ob A. S. Grine." Unpublished MS.

NNG Corr.   Correspondence of Nina Nikolaevna Grin with Vera Pavlovna Kalitskaia, 1927-1941. Unpublished MS.

Sobranie sochinenii   A. S. Grin, *Sobranie sochinenii v shesti tomakh* (Moscow: "Pravda," 1965).

VP   Vera Pavlovna Kalitskaia, "Vospominaniia ob A. S. Grine." Unpublished MS.

Archives

BL   Biblioteka imeni Lenina, Otdel rukopisei, Moscow.

IMLI   Institut Mirovoi Literatury imeni Gor'kogo (Akad. Nauk SSSR), Otdel rukopisei, Moscow.

IRLI   Institut Russkoi Literatury (Pushkinskii Dom), (Akad. Nauk SSSR), Leningrad.

TsGALI   Tsentral'nyi Gosudarstvennyi Arkhiv Literatury i Iskusstva, Moscow.

In references to archive sources, the abbreviation "ed. khr." stands for *edinitsa* (or *edinitsy*) *khraneniia*.

NOTES AND REFERENCES

Chapter I. The Early Years

1. *Sobranie sochinenii*, VI, 402, beginning of first variant of chapter "Baku" of Grin's *Avtobiograficheskaia povest'*.

2. See Vl. Sandler, ed., *Vospominaniia ob Aleksandre Grine* (Leningrad: "Lenizdat," 1972).

3. *Sobranie sochinenii*, VI, 228-361.

4. NNG.

5. See A. Likhanov, "Novye dokumenty ob Aleksandre Grine," *Kirovskaia pravda*, 19/II/1960, p. 3.

6. *Ibid.* Some commentators have suggested the possibility of a link between Grin's family and that of Joseph Conrad. As far as I have been able to ascertain, there was no contact between Stefan Grinevskii and Joseph Conrad's father, Apollo Korzeniowski, who was exiled to Vologda from Warsaw in May 1862, for underground revolutionary activities. (See G. Jean-Aubry, *Joseph Conrad, Life and Letters*, 2 vols. [London, 1927], I, pp. 6-8; and Z. Najder, *Conrad's Polish Background*, [Oxford, 1964], pp. 1-31).

7. K. Paustovskii, "Aleksandr Grin. Biografiia, 1940," IMLI, fond 95, opis' 1, ed. khr. 7, list 1. Paustovskii probably did more than any Soviet author to popularise Grin. For example, Grin appears as the writer Gart in Paustovskii's tale of the Crimea, *Chërnoe more* (1935), while the chapter of the same work entitled "Skazochnik" is devoted to Grin and to the house where he died. (See K. Paustov-. skii, *Sobranie sochinenii v vos'mi tomakh* [Moscow: Izd-vo "Khudozhestvennaia literatura," 1967-70], II, 170-73).

8. N. P. Izergina, "A. S. Grin i A. M. Gor'kii," *Uchënye zapiski*, Kafedra literatury, Kirovskii gosudarstvennyi pedagogicheskii institut imeni Lenina, Vol. XX, Kirov, 1965, p. 80.

9. *Sobranie sochinenii*, VI, 229.

10. Egl' and Assol' are central characters in Grin's novella *Alye parusa (Scarlet Sails)* (1923): Egl' is an old collector of folk tales and legends, while Assol' is the young heroine. (See *ibid.*, III, 3-65).

11. NNG.

12. *Sobranie sochinenii*, VI, 229.

13. Likhanov.

14. *Sobranie sochinenii*, VI, 230.

15. This name for the fictitious setting of Grin's romantic works was first coined by the critic K. Zelinskii in 1934 (see his article "Grin," *Krasnaia nov'*, No. 4 [1934], p. 200). Since then the term has become widely used. For an examination of *Grinlandia*, see N. J. L. Luker, "Alexander Grin's *Grinlandia*," in R. Freeborn, ed., *Russian and Slavic Literature* (Cambridge, Mass.: Slavica Publishers, 1976), pp. 190-212.

16. *Sobranie sochinenii*, VI, 231.
17. *Ibid*.
18. *Ibid*.
19. Likhanov.
20. *Sobranie sochinenii*, VI, 239.
21. *Ibid*., p. 240.
22. *Ibid*.
23. *Ibid*., pp. 243-44.
24. *Ibid*., pp. 244-45.
25. *Ibid*., p. 246.
26. *Ibid*., p. 247.
27. *Ibid*.
28. *Ibid*.
29. *Ibid*., pp. 247-48. For an account of this significant episode, see N. N. Grin, "Kratkaia biografiia A. S. Grina," IMLI, fond 95, opis' 1, ed. khr. 8, list 4.
30. *Sobranie sochinenii*, VI, 248.
31. *Ibid*., p. 250. Elsewhere Grin wrote that he undertook the journey in accordance with "the behests of Walter Scott and Gustave Aimard." ("Avtobiograficheskie ocherki," TsGALI, fond 127, opis' 1, ed. khr. 56, listy 69-70).
32. *Sobranie sochinenii*, VI, 252.
33. *Ibid*., p. 254.
34. *Ibid*., p. 255.
35. *Ibid*., p. 256.
36. *Ibid*.
37. *Ibid*., p. 266.
38. See *ibid*., V, 3-182.
39. See *ibid*., VI, 278-80.
40. *Ibid*., p. 280.
41. See *ibid*., pp. 3-227.
42. *Ibid*., p. 289.
43. *Ibid*.
44. *Ibid*., p. 299.
45. *Ibid*., p. 304.
46. See *ibid*., II, 77-83.
47. A. S. Grin, "Avtobiograficheskie ocherki," TsGALI, fond 127, opis' 1, ed. khr. 56, list 16.
48. *Sobranie sochinenii*, VI, 321.
49. *Ibid*., p. 324.
50. *Ibid*., p. 327. Grin's impressions of the goldfields are contained in his autobiographical sketch *Zoloto i shakhtëry* (1925). See FD, 534-40.
51. *Sobranie sochinenii*, VI, 339.
52. See DM, 128-30.
53. *Ibid*., p. 129.
54. See Vl. Sandler, "Grin, kotorogo vy ne znaete," *Volga*, No. 8 (1967), p. 157.
55. *Ibid*.
56. NNG.
57. DM, 130.
58. NNG.

59. VP.

60. See *Sobranie sochinenii*, I, 121-52.

61. Grin's tale *Tretii etazh* is dedicated to him (see *Sobranie sochinenii*, I, 170-78, 458). For references to Bykhovskii, see Oliver H. Radkey, *The Agrarian Foes of Bolshevism* (New York: Columbia Univ. Press, 1958).

62. VP.

63. See *Sobranie sochinenii*, I, 54-66.

64. See *ibid*., pp. 191-96.

65. *Ibid*., VI, 344.

66. NNG.

67. *Ibid*.

68. See Sandler, "Grin, kotorogo vy ne znaete," *Volga*, No. 9 (1967), p. 136.

69. *Ibid*., pp. 140-41.

70. See *Sobranie sochinenii*, VI, 350.

71. Sandler.

72. N. N. Nikandrov, "Vospominaniia ob A. S. Grine." Unpublished MS. in private hands in USSR.

73. The complete manuscript of the tale is believed to have been lost in the early 1920s by the *Raduga* ("Rainbow") publishing house. However, what is thought to be a fragment of it has survived. See "Pamiati leitenanta Shmidta," *Raduga*, No. 8 (1965), p. 121.

74. See Sandler, "Chetyre goda za Grinom," *Al'manakh Prometei* (Moscow: "Molodaia gvardiia," 1968), p. 191.

75. Originally head of the local SR cell in Sevastopol', Ekaterina Bibergal' was later sentenced to a long term of hard labour in Siberia, and she and Grin probably never met again.

76. See Sandler, p. 193.

77. VP.

78. See *Sobranie sochinenii*, I, 431-44.

79. Sandler, p. 195.

80. See *Sobranie sochinenii*, II, 133-69.

81. See BS, 47-80. Grin's title echoes that of Krylov's fable.

82. See *Sobranie sochinenii*, I, 37-45.

83. See note, *ibid*., p. 456. Besides the two pseudonyms quoted, "A. A. –v" and his most frequent "A. S. Grin," Grin is also known to have used the following: Grin, A.; Grin, A. S.; Grin, Aleksandr; Klemm, Viktoriia; M–v, A.; Moravskaia, El'za; and Stepanov. In addition, he may also have used: Grinevich; Sasha Grigor'ev; and V. Grin. (See I. F. Masanov, *Slovar' psevdonimov russkikh pisatelei*, 4 vols. [Moscow: "Vsesoiuznaia knizhnaia palata," 1956-60], I, 305; IV, 147).

84. See *Novoe slovo*, No. 11 (1909), pp. 33-40.

85. See *Sobranie sochinenii*, I, 85-92. The tale almost certainly reflects the beginning of Grin's relationship with Vera Pavlovna and their secret correspondence during his imprisonment early in 1906.

86. See *ibid*., pp. 93-97.

87. See *ibid*., pp. 98-102.

88. NNG.

89. VP.

90. See *Sobranie sochinenii*, I, 67-84.

91. Sandler, p. 201.
92. St. Petersburg ("Nasha zhizn'"), 1908.
93. See *Sobranie sochinenii*, I, 250-71.
94. NNG.
95. Izergina is inaccurate in dating this letter 1907. See Izergina, p. 83.
96. See *sbornik* A. S. Grin, *Chërnyi almaz* (Leningrad: "Mysl'," 1928), pp. 27-70.
97. See FD, 170-207.
98. See *Sobranie sochinenii*, I, 315-66.
99. See *ibid*., pp. 374-79.
100. See *ibid*., II, 48-54.
101. Now part of tale *Nasledstvo Pik-Mika*, *Sobranie sochinenii*, III, 333-35.
102. Now part of *ibid*., pp. 331-33.
103. Now entitled *Vozvrashchenie "Chaiki"*, *ibid*., II, 15-27.
104. See A. G. Gornfel'd, "A. Grin: *Rasskazy*, SPb., 1910," *Russkoe bogatstvo*, No. 3 (1910), pp. 145-47.
105. See N. Verzhbitskii, "Svetlaia dusha," *Nash sovremennik*, No. 8 (1964), p. 103.
106. Sandler, p. 205.
107. *Ibid*.
108. *Ibid*.
109. Of his father's advice at the time to plead for clemency, Grin wrote: "I was ready to die rather than do that." (*Sobranie sochinenii*, VI, 356).
110. Sandler, p. 206.
111. For details, see N. N. Grin, "Kratkaia biografiia A. S. Grina," TsGALI, fond 127, opis' 1, ed. khr. 167, list 4.

Chapter II. Archangel, Petersburg and Petrograd

1. I. V. Myl'tsina, "A. S. Grin v arkhangel'skoi ssylke." Unpublished MS. in private hands in USSR.
2. E. I. Studentsova, "Vospominaniia ob A. S. Grine," TsGALI, fond 127, opis' 3, ed. khr. 11, list 5.
3. See FD, 293-356.
4. NNG.
5. O. Voronova, "Sto vërst po zhizni," *Baikal*, No. 4 (1967), p. 147.
6. See *Sobranie sochinenii*, II, 84-115.
7. See *ibid*., pp. 116-32.
8. VP.
9. M. O. Mashintseva and A. D. Fedotova-Petrova, "Vospominaniia ob A. S. Grine." Unpublished MS. in private hands in USSR.
10. See *Sobranie sochinenii*, III, 382-409.
11. VP.
12. *Ibid*.
13. *Ibid*.

14. See *Sobranie sochinenii*, III, 403.

15. VP.

16. *Ibid.*

17. NNG Corr. Letter to Vera Pavlovna Kalitskaia, 28 April 1932.

18. NNG.

19. *Ibid.*

20. VP.

21. IRLI, *Arkhiv Andreeva*, fond 9, opis' 3, ed. khr. 14, list 1.

22. NNG.

23. I. Sokolov-Mikitov, "Chelovek iz Zurbagana." Unpublished MS. in private hands in USSR.

24. See, for example, BL, fond 245, karton No. 6, ed. khr. 16, letter from Grin to Larissa Mikhailovna Reisner and Mikhail Andreevich Reisner, 8 December 1915.

25. See Vl. Sandler, "Slezhka za A. Grinom," *Molodaia gvardiia*, No. 10 (1965), pp. 166-67.

26. BL, *Izdatel'stvo A. F. Marksa*, karton No. 1, ed. khr. 27, list 3.

27. IRLI, *Arkhiv Miroliubova*, fond 185, opis' 1, ed. khr. 453, undated.

28. L. Lesnaia-Shperling, "Aleksandr Grin v *Satirikone*." Unpublished MS. in private hands in USSR.

29. See *Sobranie sochinenii*, IV, 136-43.

30. See *ibid.*, pp. 174-78.

31. See *ibid.*, pp. 179-89.

32. See *Dvadtsatyi vek*, No. 35 (1916), p. 5.

33. See FD, 523-29.

34. *Ibid.*, p. 523.

35. NNG.

36. See *Sobranie sochinenii*, III, 427-31.

37. NNG.

38. TsGALI, fond 127, opis' 1, ed. khr. 215, list 4.

39. *Ibid.*, list 3. For a translation of both and short afterword, see N. J. L. Luker, *Russian Literature Triquarterly*, No. 11, (Winter, 1975), pp. 88-94.

40. See *Sovetskaia Ukraina*, No. 8 (1960), p. 103.

41. See *Chërtovaia perechnitsa*, No. 7 (1918), p. 2.

42. See *Vsevidiashchee oko*, No. 1 (1918), pp. 3-4.

43. See Vl. Sandler, "Kak priplyli k nam *Alye parusa*," *Krymskaia pravda*, 7/I/1966, p. 4.

44. Grin's *Trudovaia knizhka* of 1921, after his marriage to his second wife, shows him as being married only twice (TsGALI, fond 127, opis' 1, ed. khr. 164, list 16).

45. NNG.

46. *Ibid.*

47. IRLI, R.I., opis' 5, No. 384.

48. NNG. The brief quotations which follow in the same paragraph derive from the same source.

49. *Ibid.*

50. See A. G. Gornfel'd, "A. Grin, *Rasskazy*, SPb., 1910," *Russkoe bogatstvo*, No. 3 (1910), pp. 145-47.

51. A. G. Gornfel'd, "A. G., *Iskatel' prikliuchenii*, M., 1916," *ibid.*, Nos. 6-7 (1917), pp. 279-82.

52. NNG.

53. See *Plamia*, No. 36 (1919), pp. 11-15.

54. See *ibid.*, No. 46 (1919), pagination unclear.

55. See *ibid.*, No. 64 (1919), p. 2.

56. See *ibid.*, No. 39 (1919), p. 9.

57. NNG.

58. Anna Vivanti, *I Divoratori* (Milan, 1911). The translated title *Poglotiteli* is given by Nina Grin (NNG). I have been unable to find any record of this Russian translation.

59. NNG.

60. *Ibid.*

61. See *Sobranie sochinenii*, IV, 358-92.

62. See *ibid.*, V, 345-98.

63. See Grin's *Fandango, ibid.*, p. 345.

64. Today the whole building still stands and the upper floor, with its windows looking out on to the Moika, is unchanged, but the ground floor where the bank once was is now occupied by shops, offices, a café and a cinema. The original façade of the bank is, however, largely preserved. For a detailed and informative account of the House of Arts and similar institutions in Petrograd, see Barry Scherr, "Notes on Literary Life in Petrograd, 1918-1922: A Tale of Three Houses," *Slavic Review*, 36, No. 2 (June 1977), pp. 256-67.

65. See BS, 269-386.

66. TsGALI, fond 127, opis' 1, ed. khr. 26, listy 1-87.

67. See O. Forsh, *Sumasshedshii korabl'* (Washington, D.C.: Inter-Language Literary Associates, 1964). In his foreword to this edition (pp. 7-55), Boris Filippov deciphers many of the pseudonyms used by the author for the inhabitants of *Dom iskusstv*.

68. Vl. Khodasevich, *Literaturnye stat'i i vospominaniia* (New York: Chekhov Publishing House, 1954), p. 406.

69. See Izergina.

70. *Alye parusa* (Moscow-Petrograd: Izd-vo L. D. Frenkel', 1923).

71. Vl. Sandler, "Kak priplyli k nam *Alye parusa*" (ii), *Krymskaia pravda*, 7/I/1966, p. 4.

72. M. Slonimskii, "A. S. Grin," introductory article to A. S. Grin, *Zolotaia tsep'; Avtobiograficheskaia povest'* (Moscow: "Sovetskii pisatel'," 1939), p. 27.

73. NNG.

74. N. N. Grin, "Kratkaia biografiia A. S. Grina," TsGALI, fond 127, opis' 1, ed. khr. 167, list 5.

75. IMLI, *Arkhiv Gor'kogo*, B10, 21, 3, 10, list 1.

76. NNG.

77. *Ibid.*

78. N. N. Grin, letter to V. I. Borshchukov from Staryi Krym, 6 December 1961 (IMLI, fond 95, opis' 1, ed. khr. 11, list 4).

Chapter III. The Last Years

1. TsGALI, fond 127, opis' 1, ed. khr. 28, list 1.
2. NNG.
3. See *Sobranie sochinenii*, IV, 269-74.
4. See *ibid.*, III, 432-37.
5. NNG.
6. *Ibid.*
7. See *Mukhomor*, No. 4 (1922), p. 3.
8. See *ibid.*, No. 5 (1922), p. 3.
9. See *ibid.*, No. 7 (1922), p. 3.
10. See *Sobranie sochinenii*, IV, 282-87.
11. See *ibid.*, pp. 243-61.
12. See *ibid.*, pp. 308-12.
13. And *not* in 1925, in No. 24 of *Krasnaia niva* (*Sobranie sochinenii*, V, 476, note). See I. Sukiasova, "Novoe ob Aleksandre Grine," *Literaturnaia Gruziia*, No. 12 (1968), pp. 67-76.
14. See *Sobranie sochinenii*, II, 372-404.
15. See *ibid.*, pp. 332-40.
16. See *ibid.*, III, 336-55.
17. See letter from Grin to A. I. Svirskii, 19 July 1923 (IMLI, fond 78, opis' 1, ed. khr. 30, list 1).
18. This fascinating and highly revealing manuscript is held by TsGALI but not released even to Soviet researchers. A copy was read in private hands in the USSR.
19. NNG.
20. *Ibid.*
21. See *Sobranie sochinenii*, IV, 3-125.
22. NNG.
23. *Ibid.*
24. See *Sobranie sochinenii*, V, 3-182. The work's title may well have been inspired by *The Skimmer of the Seas*, the sub-title of Fenimore Cooper's novel *The Water-Witch* (1831). Cooper's works were widely available in Russian translation by the late 1800s and Grin appears to have been familiar with several of them.
25. NNG.
26. *Ibid.*
27. *Ibid.*
28. *Ibid.*
29. *Ibid.*
30. See DM, 372-491; also FD, 5-162. For an examination of this much-neglected work, see N. J. L. Luker, "Alexander Grin's *Jessy and Morgiana:* Literary Lapse or New Departure?," *Journal of Russian Studies*, No. 35 (1978), pp. 16-21.
31. See *Sobranie sochinenii*, V, 399-404.
32. See *ibid.*, pp. 415-19.
33. See *ibid.*, pp. 409-14.
34. See postcard from unknown correspondent to A. S. and N. N. Grin at Kislovodsk, dated 31 May 1927 (TsGALI, fond 127, opis' 1, ed. khr. 111, list 1, ob.)

35. NNG.

36. In Feodosia (TsGALI, fond 127, opis' 1, ed. khr. 21, list 88).

37. NNG.

38. According to Nina Grin (NNG), Vol'fson also agreed to buy the collected works of Sergeev-Tsenskii. (See her "Kratkaia biografiia A. S. Grina," IMLI, fond 95, opis' 1, ed. khr. 8, list 22.)

39. Their titles were to have been: 1, *Dezirada* (first variant of title *Begushchaia po volnam*); 3, *Blistaiushchii mir*; 4, *Ogon' i voda*; 7, *Prokhodnoi dvor*; 9, *Tretii etazh*; 10, *Fandango*; and 15, *Otblesk mecha*. See A. M. Gurvich and Vl. M. Rossel's, "Grin, A., *Bibliograficheskii ukazatel'* (Moscow, 1960), p. 15. This index is unpublished and held in typescript by the Bibliography Department of the Lenin Library, Moscow.

40. Grin's tale *Vetka omely* is dedicated to him (see *Sobranie sochinenii*, V, 465-71, 478).

41. NNG Corr. Letter to Vera Pavlovna from Feodosia, 3 June 1930.

42. *Ibid.* Letter to Vera Pavlovna from Moscow, 8 July 1930.

43. For example: short variant of *Doroga nikuda* in MS. of *Dzhessi i Morgiana* (TsGALI, fond 127, opis' 1, ed. khr. 21, list 76). Also, rough variants of *Dzhessi i Morgiana* contain fragments of *Doroga nikuda* (TsGALI, fond 127, opis' 1, ed. khr. 24, list 77).

44. Vera Pavlovna is, however, slightly inaccurate here, as Grin's last novel was not given its present title until the following summer, 1928.

45. VP.

46. Yorkshire art teacher and author (1885-1954). See his *The Dales are Mine* (London: Skeffington, 1952), p. 96, for the engraving of "The Road to Nowhere."

47. NNG.

48. *Ibid.*

49. *Ibid.*

50. See *Vsemirnyi sledopyt*, No. 2 (1930), pp. 146-52.

51. See *Sobranie sochinenii*, VI, 394-98.

52. See *Vokrug sveta*, No. 30 (1930), pp. 21-23.

53. In Nos. 2, 3, 4 and 9.

54. See *Sobranie sochinenii*, VI, 371-77.

55. See *ibid.*, pp. 385-93.

56. See *ibid.*, pp. 362-70.

57. In *Krasnaia nov'*, No. 5 (1933), pp. 174-86.

58. NNG.

59. *Ibid.*

60. *Ibid.*

61. *Ibid.*

62. *Ibid.* The *Arkhiv Gor'kogo* (IMLI) did not release this letter with others from Grin to Gor'kii.

63. NNG.

64. *Ibid.*

65. See note, *Sobranie sochinenii*, VI, 399.

66. Ts. Vol'pe, "Ob avantiurno-psikhologicheskikh novellakh A. Grina," foreword to A. Grin, *Rasskazy* (Leningrad: Izd-vo "Pisatelei v Leningrade," 1935), pp. 6-7.

67. NNG.
68. *Ibid.*
69. *Ibid.*
70. NNG Corr.
71. *Ibid.*
72. See "Nabroski vtoroi glavy *Nedotrogi*," *Literaturnoe nasledstvo*, Vol. 74 (Moscow: "Nauka," 1965), pp. 654-67; also explanation of same by N. N. Grin, pp. 667-68; *Istoriia Degzha* (excerpt), *Tridtsats dnei*, No. 3 (1935), pp. 17-28; *Nedotroga* (excerpt), *Ogonëk*, Nos. 2-3 (1936), p. 10, p. 22; and TsGALI, fond 127, opis' 1, ed. khr. 14-18.
73. N. N. Grin, "Ob"iasnenie k otryvkam iz poslednego romana A. Grina *Nedotroga*," *Literaturnoe nasledstvo*, Vol. 74 (Moscow: "Nauka," 1965), p. 667.
74. NNG.
75. See FD, 412-520.
76. NNG.
77. See *Ogonëk*, No. 34 (1929), pp. 6-7.
78. NNG.
79. *Ibid.*
80. IMLI, fond 95, opis' 1, ed. khr. 5, listy 2-3.
81. NNG Corr.
82. NNG.
83. *Ibid.*
84. TsGALI, fond 127, opis' 1, ed. khr. 15, list 8, ob.
85. NNG.
86. *Ibid.*
87. N. N. Grin, "Ob"iasnenie k otryvkam iz poslednego romana A. Grina *Nedotroga*," *loc. cit.*, p. 668.
88. NNG Corr., letter of 8 May 1932.
89. NNG.
90. *Ibid.*
91. NNG Corr., letter of 3 October 1932.
92. NNG Corr.
93. *Ibid.*

Epilogue

1. IMLI, *Arkhiv Gor'kogo*, PG-RL, 2, 12. Letter to N. Aseev, 1928.
2. See notes 50 and 51 for chapter 2.
3. For a more detailed treatment of dream and fantasy in Grin, see N. J. L. Luker, "Alexander Grin: A Survey," *Russian Literature Triquarterly*, No. 8 (Winter, 1974), pp. 341-59.
4. TsGALI, fond 127, opis' 1, ed. khr. 29, list 25.
5. *Sobranie sochinenii*, III, 61.
6. See A. F. Britikov, *Russkii sovetskii nauchno-fantasticheskii roman* (Leningrad: "Nauka," 1970), pp. 83-89.

7. See Iu. Olesha, *Izbrannye sochineniia* (Moscow: "Khud. lit.," 1956), p. 464.

8. V. Vazhdaev, "Propovednik kosmopolitizma; Nechistyi smysl 'chistogo is-kusstva' Aleksandra Grina," *Novyi mir*, No. 1 (1950), pp. 257-72.

9. A. Tarasenkov, "O natsional'nykh traditsiiakh i burzhuaznom kosmopoli-tizme," *Znamia*, No. 1 (1950), pp. 152-64.

10. For an examination of the Utopian genre in nineteenth-century Russian lit-erature, see L. M. Lotman, *Realizm russkoi literatury 60kh godov XIX veka* (Len-ingrad: "Nauka," 1974), pp. 207-56. For a list of studies of the genre in several languages, see *ibid.*, p. 211. An examination of Soviet Utopianism can be found in Bernd Rullkötter's recent study of Soviet science fiction, *Die wissenschaftliche Phantastik der Sowjetunion* (Bern and Frankfurt-am-Main: Herbert and Peter Lang, 1974), pp. 62-114.

11. M. Shcheglov, "Korabli Aleksandra Grina," *Novyi mir*, No. 10 (1956), pp. 220-23.

12. *Ibid.*, p. 223.

13. V. Zavalishin, *Early Soviet Writers* (New York: Praeger, 1958), p. 317.

14. Elizabeth K. Beaujour, *The Invisible Land: A Study of the Artistic Imagi-nation of Iurii Olesha* (New York: Columbia Univ. Press, 1970), p. 166.

15. *Ibid.*, p. 167.

16. N. N. Grin, "Kratkaia biografiia A. S. Grina," IMLI, fond 95, opis' 1, ed. khr. 8, list 17.

17. *Ibid.*

18. NNG.

BIBLIOGRAPHY

The sources given in Section B below should be supplemented by the more comprehensive bibliography of Grin compiled by N. J. L. Luker, in Fred Moody, ed., *10 Bibliographies of 20th Century Russian Literature* (Ann Arbor, Mich.: Ardis, 1977), pp. 103-18.

A.   *Unpublished Sources*
(i)   Memoir Material.
   Copies of the following MSS. in private hands were consulted in the Soviet Union. The originals of several of these, notably those by N. N. Grin and V. P. Kalitskaia, are known to be held by TsGALI, although its *Putevoditel'* (see below) does not actually say so. The Archive would not release any of the memoirs listed below.

Arnol'di, E. M.,   "Aleksandr Grin, Belletrist."
Verzhbitskii, N.,   "Svetlaia dusha."
Grin, N. N.,   "Grin i vino."
Grin, N. N.,   "Zapiski ob A. S. Grine."
Grin, N. N.,   Correspondence with Vera Pavlovna Kalitskaia, 1927-1941.
Kalitskaia, V. P.,   "Vospominaniia ob A. S. Grine."
Kremlëv, I.,   "Kaprizy slavy."
Lesnaia-Shperling, L.,   "Aleksandr Grin v *Satirikone*."
Mashintseva, M. O., i
Fedotova-Petrova, A. D.,   "Vospominaniia ob A. S. Grine."
Nikandrov, N. N.,   "Vospominaniia ob A. S. Grine."
Sokolov-Mikitov, I.,   "Chelovek iz Zurbagana."
Shklovskii, V.,   "O Grine."

(ii)   Archive Material.
   All main archives in the USSR with holdings on Grin were consulted for this study. These were:
Biblioteka imeni Lenina, Otdel Rukopisei, Moscow. Entries under Grin in card index.
Institut Mirovoi Literatury imeni Gor'kogo, Arkhiv Gor'kogo, Moscow, (Akad. Nauk SSSR).
   Holding numbers: KG-P 22 3 1; KG-P 22 3 3; KG-P 22 3 4;
                     KG-P 22 3 6; B10 21 3 10; KG-RZN 1 129 1.
Institut Mirovoi Literatury imeni Gor'kogo, Otdel Rukopisei, Moscow, (Akad. Nauk SSSR).
   Holding numbers: Fond 95, opis' 1, edinitsy khraneniia 1-22, (1908-1962).
                    Also Fond 15, opis' 2; Fond 56, opis' 1; Fond 78, opis' 1, No. 30.

Institut Russkoi Literatury (Pushkinskii Dom), Leningrad, (Akad. Nauk SSSR). Entries under Grin in card index.
Tsentral'nyi Gosudarstvennyi Arkhiv Literatury i Iskusstva, Moscow.
Holding numbers: Fond 127, 307 edinitsy khraneniia, (1907-1941).

Reference works about archive holdings:
Lichnye Arkhivnye Fondy v Gosudarstvennykh Khranilishchakh SSSR. Ukazatel', 2 vols. (Moscow: GAU pri Sov. Min. SSSR, 1962-63). For Grin: I, 209.
Tsentral'nyi Gosudarstvennyi Arkhiv Literatury i Iskusstva (TsGALI), *Putevoditel' po literaturnym fondam* (Moscow: GAU pri Sov. Min. SSSR, 1963). For Grin: p. 153; Vypusk 3 (Moscow: 1968), p. 417 (addenda).

B.   *Published Sources*
(i)   Major recent collections of Grin's work.
Sobranie sochinenii v shesti tomakh (Moscow: "Pravda," 1965).
Belyi shar (Rasskazy i povesti) (Moscow: "Molodaia gvardiia," 1966).
Dzhessi i Morgiana (Povest', novelly, roman) (Leningrad: "Lenizdat," 1966).
Fandango (Roman, povesti i rasskazy. Avtobiograficheskie ocherki) (Simferopol': Izd-vo "Krym," 1966).
Izbrannoe (Simferopol': Izd-vo "Krym," 1969).
Alye parusa (Izbrannye proizvedeniia) (Leningrad: "Lenizdat," 1972).

(ii) Works by Grin in translation.
(a) English.
"The Making of Asper," in *Dissonant Voices in Soviet Literature*, ed. Patricia Blake and Max Hayward (London: Allen and Unwin, 1964), pp. 61-72.
Scarlet Sails, tr. T. Whitney (New York: Charles Scribner's Sons, 1967).
"The Watercolour," tr. M. Wheeler, in *Soviet Short Stories*, No. 2 (London: Penguin, 1968), pp. 95-107.
"Peace," tr. N. J. L. Luker, *New Zealand Slavonic Journal*, No. 1 (1974), · p. 87-99.
"The Snake," "The Voice of the Siren," "The Window in the Forest," tr. N. J. L. Luker, *Russian Literature Triquarterly*, No. 8 (1974), pp. 177-88.
"The Garrulous Gremlin," tr. R. W. Rotsel, *ibid.*, pp. 188-91.
"The Corpses" and "Red Splashes of Blood," tr. N. J. L. Luker, *ibid.*, No. 11 (1975), pp. 88-94.
(b) French.
Celle qui Court sur les Vagues, tr. Jacques Croisé and Armand Pierhal (Paris: Robert Laffont, 1959).
L'Attrapeur de Rats, tr. Paul Castaing (Lausanne: Editions l'Age d'-Homme, 1972).
(c) German.
Die purpurroten Segel, (with "Der Schandpfahl," "Der ratlose Hausgeist," "Das Aquarell," "Der Zorn des Vaters," and "Der Hafenkapitän"), tr. Elena Guttenberger (Frankfurt-am-Main: Possev), 1967.
Jessy und Morgiana, Roman, tr. Eva und Alexander Grossmann (Weimar: Kiepenhauer, 1967).

(iii) Studies containing biographical information.

Kharchev, V. V., *Poeziia i proza Aleksandra Grina* (Gor'kii: "Volgo-Viatskoe kn. izd-vo," 1975).

Kovskii, V. E., *Romanticheskii mir Aleksandra Grina* (Moscow: "Nauka," 1969).

Luker, N. J. L., *Alexander Grin* (Letchworth, England: Bradda Books, 1973).

Mikhailova, L., *Aleksandr Grin* (Moscow: "Khudozhestvennaia literatura," 1972).

Prokhorov, E. I., *Aleksandr Grin* (Moscow: "Prosveshchenie," 1970).

Sandler, Vl., ed., *Vospominaniia ob Aleksandre Grine* (Leningrad: "Lenizdat," 1972).

(iv) Essays and articles.

Arnol'di, E., "Belletrist Grin. Vstrechi s pisatelem," *Zvezda*, No. 12 (1963), pp. 176-82.

Borisov, L., "Aleksandr Grin i ego tvorchestvo," in A. S. Grin, *Begushchaia po volnam* (Moscow-Leningrad: "Detskaia literatura," 1945), pp. 3-8.

Grin, N. N., "Ob"iasnenie k otryvkam iz poslednego romana A. Grina *Nedotroga*," *Literaturnoe nasledstvo*, 74 (Moscow: "Nauka," 1965), pp. 667-68.

Grin, N. N., "Zapiski ob A. S. Grine," *Literaturnaia Rossiia*, No. 34 (1970), pp. 12-13, p. 22.

Izergina, N. P., "A. S. Grin i A. M. Gor'kii," *Uchënye zapiski*, Kafedra literatury, Kirovskii gosud. ped. inst. im. Lenina, 20 (Kirov, 1965), pp. 78-108.

Kalitskaia, V. P., "Mechtatel'," *Kostër*, No. 10 (1945), pp. 10-11.

Konichev, K., "Dokumenty rasskazyvaiut," *Pravda severa*, 6/IX/1964, pp. 3-4.

Lidin, Vl., "Aleksandr Grin," *Moskva*, No. 10 (1963), pp. 164-65.

Luker, N. J. L., "Alexander Grin: A Survey," *Russian Literature Triquarterly*, No. 8 (1974), pp. 341-59.

Mal'tsev, S. i Turintsev, A., "Tobolskaia nakhodka. Novye dokumenty ob Aleksandre Grine," *Pravda vostoka*, 12/II/1964, p. 4.

Olesha, Iu., "Aleksandr Grin," *Izbrannye sochineniia* (Moscow: "Khud. lit.," 1956), pp. 463-67.

Paustovskii, K., "Zhizn' Grina," foreword to A. Grin, *Zolotaia tsep'; Avtobiograficheskaia povest'* (Moscow: "Sovetskii pisatel'," 1939), pp. 3-24. (The first of many similar introductory essays.)

Paustovskii, K., "Arkhangel'skie nakhodki," *Literaturnaia gazeta*, 29/VIII/1964, p. 1.

Rossel's, Vl., "Dorevoliutsionnaia proza Grina," in A. S. Grin, *Sobranie sochinenii v shesti tomakh* (Moscow: "Pravda," 1965), I, 445-53.

Rossel's, Vl., "A. Grin. Iz neizdannogo i zabytogo," *Literaturnoe nasledstvo*, 74 (Moscow: "Nauka," 1965), pp. 629-48.

Rossel's, Vl., "A. S. Grin," *Istoriia russkoi sovetskoi literatury*, 4 vols. (Moscow: "Nauka," 1967-71), I, 370-91.

Rozhdestvenskii, Vs., "Dom iskusstv," in *Stranitsy zhizni; Iz literaturnykh vospominanii* (Moscow-Leningrad: "Sovetskii pisatel'," 1962), pp. 201-03.

Sandler, Vl., "Samyi pervyi," *Literaturnaia Rossiia*, No. 35 (1964), p. 8.

Sandler, Vl., "Slezhka za A. Grinom," *Molodaia gvardiia*, No. 10 (1965), pp. 166-67.

Sandler, Vl., "Kak priplyli k nam *Alye parusa*" (i), *Krymskaia pravda*, 6/I/1966, p. 4; (ii), 7/I/1966, p. 4.

Sandler, Vl., "Shël po zemle mechtatel'," foreword to A. S. Grin, *Dzhessi i Morgiana* (Leningrad: "Lenizdat," 1966), pp. 3-20.

Sandler, Vl., "O cheloveke i pisatele," foreword to A. S. Grin, *Belyi shar* (Moscow: "Molodaia gvardiia," 1966), pp. 3-25.

Sandler, Vl., "Grin, kotorogo vy ne znaete" (i), *Volga*, No. 8 (1967), pp. 155-72; (ii), No. 9 (1967), pp. 136-48.

Sandler, Vl., "Chetyre goda za Grinom," Al'manakh *Prometei*, V (Moscow, 1968), pp. 190-207.

Sandler, Vl., "Arkhangel'skaia odisseia Aleksandra Grina," *Sever*, No. 8 (1969), pp. 97-114.

Sandler, Vl., "V poiskakh Aleksandra Grina," *Kodry*, No. 8 (1970), pp. 121-29.

Scherr, B., "Aleksandr Grin's *Scarlet Sails* and the Fairy Tale," *Slavic and East European Journal*, 20, No. 4 (1976), pp. 387-99.

Shcheglov, M., "Korabli Aleksandra Grina," *Novyi mir*, No. 10 (1956), pp. 220-23.

Shklovskii, V., "Ledokhod," *Kodry*, No. 11 (1971), pp. 88-89.

Slonimskii, M., "Aleksandr Grin," *Zvezda*, No. 4 (1939), pp. 159-67.

Slonimskii, M., "A. S. Grin," foreword to A. Grin, *Zolotaia tsep'; Avtobiograficheskaia povest'* (Moscow: "Sovetskii pisatel'," 1939), pp. 24-35.

Slonimskii, M., "Ob avtore *Alykh parusov*," foreword to Grin's *Chetyre ginei, Zvezda*, No. 9 (1960), p. 215.

Smirenskii, V., "Vstrechi s pisateliami—Aleksandr Grin," *Don* (Rostov), No. 12 (1957), pp. 170-73.

Sukiasova, I., "Novoe ob Aleksandre Grine," *Literaturnaia Gruziia*, No. 12 (1968), pp. 67-76.

Tkalich, D., "Stranitsy iz zhizni A. Grina," *Ural*, No. 8 (1967), pp. 186-87.

Tolstaia, A., "Aleksandr Grin. Ego *Reka*—Severnaia Dvina," *Den' poezii severa*, 1967, Petrozavodsk (pub. 1968), pp. 137-39.

Vakhtin, B., "V Starom Krymu," *Neva*, No. 8 (1960), pp. 151-54.

Verzhbitskii, N., "Svetlaia dusha," *Nash sovremennik*, No. 8 (1964), pp. 103-06.

Vikhrov, V., "A. S. Grin v *Novom Satirikone*," *Krymskaia pravda*, 18/VII/1965, p. 4.

Vikhrov, V., "Rytsar' mechty," foreword to A. S. Grin, *Sobranie sochinenii v shesti tomakh*, I, 3-36.

INDEX
(Works by Grin are listed under his name)